MENDIP'S PAST

A Shared Inheritance

Penny Stokes

MENDIP
DISTRICT COUNCIL

in association with Somerset Books

First published in Great Britain in 1999

© Penny Stokes and Mendip District Council,
reserving the copyright of the illustrations listed
in Acknowledgements to the individual contributors,
1999

British Library Cataloguing in Publication Data
A catalogue record for this book is available from The British Library

ISBN 0 861834 95 X

Trade sales and enquiries:
Somerset Books, Halsgrove House, Lower Moor Way, Tiverton, EX16 6SS
Tel: 01884 243242 Fax: 01884 243325

Printed in England by Doveton Press Limited, Bristol

CONTENTS

LIST OF ILLUSTRATIONS

COLOUR PLATES

ACKNOWLEDGEMENTS

Thanks are due to the many people who have contributed to this book both directly, by giving help and advice, and indirectly, by engaging in research in the area. I would especially like to thank Mick Aston, Bob Croft, Charles Hollinrake and John Gibson.

The line drawings have been produced by DAP; illustrations **1, 4, 5, 7, 17, 22, 23, 25, 28, 29, 31, 40, 48, 53, 55, 57, 58, 60, 69, 70, 71** and colour plates **A, B, C, D, E, F, H, I, J, K, L** and **M** are by the author. The photographs on the cover and on page 10, together with colour plate **N** are by my colleague Martin Lofthouse; **32, 34, 39** and **43** are from Mendip District Council's general stock of photographs; all other photographs are by the author unless mentioned below. Acknowledgements for illustrations are as follows: the photograph of Mick Aston, from a *Time Team* picture by Chris Bennett; **3**, from H.E. Balch's book *The Great Cave of Wookey*; **8**, drawn by Lizzie Induni, Somerset Archaeological and Natural History Society (SANHS hereafter); **20, 37, 42, 65, 66** and **67**, SANHS; **9**, West Air Photography; **10** and **12**, Tanya Cottrell; **13** and **14**, Glastonbury Antiquarian Society; **18**, Roger Leech; **21**, Bob Williams; **41**, Joyce Jefferson; **62** and **63**, and plate **G**, Wells Museum; **35** and **36**, Tony Scrase; **51**, Frome Museum; **54**, after Martin Bodman; **59** and **64**, Ian Powlesland; **61**, Gerald Quartley; **68**, Fred Davis.

FOREWORD

Mendip has a wealth of archaeological sites and historic landscapes. I live at the west end near Winscombe, and spend a great deal of the little free time I have walking in the area and visiting sites of all periods. It really is an amazing bit of country.

 I have now spent 10 years making television programmes for Channel 4 which attempt to interest everyone in the past - not just the great buildings and famous monuments but the everyday aspects that we are all familiar with, but which are no less valuable or significant just because they are local.

This book shows just what there is to see and appreciate in Mendip. The story told is not only about kings and bishops; there is more about the labour of ordinary folk - putting up buildings, ploughing the land, felling the trees and engaging in industrial activities.

I feel sure that it will increase our awareness of the historical riches around us; I hope it enables more people to get as much enjoyment and appreciation of the heritage of Mendip as I do.

Mick Aston of Channel 4's *Time Team*
Professor of Landscape Archaeology, University of Bristol

Map of Mendip District

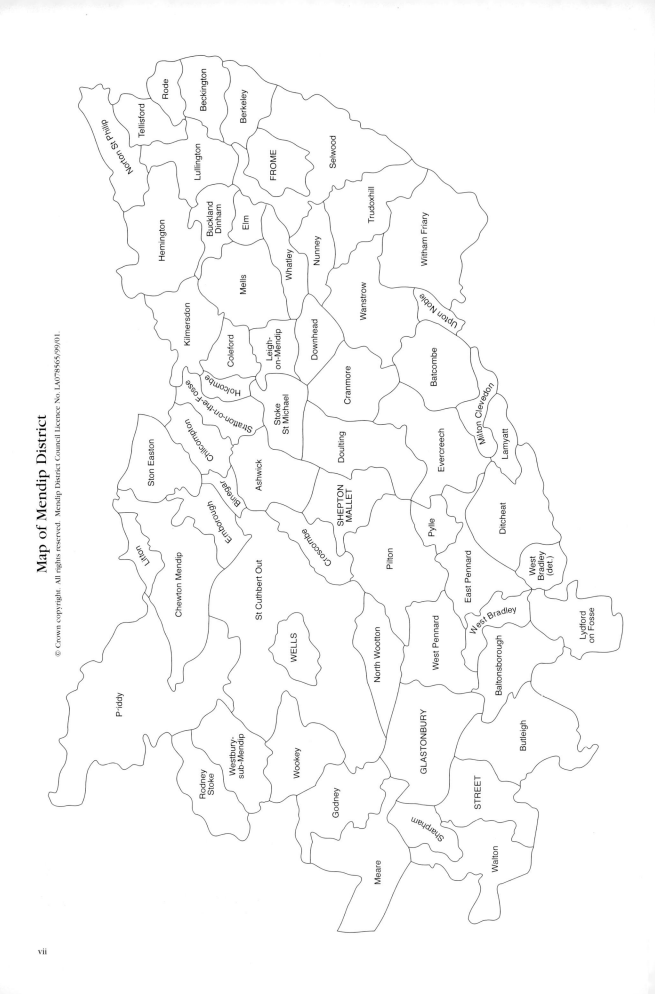

CHAPTER 1

MENDIP'S HERITAGE

Mendip District is a special place. Its specialness lies in its people, with their strong sense of community and local loyalty; in its cultural inheritance of traditions, arts, and technologies; in its natural physical character, with its extraordinary diversity of rocks, soils and landforms; and in its historic heritage of buildings, settlements and countryside, which are documents of Mendip's past.

The story of Mendip is unique. We share parts of our story with other places - national events and trends have left their mark - but the whole story of our landscape and communities is ours alone. Much of the story is still to be recovered, and much has already been lost. This book is an attempt not only to share some of what is known about Mendip's past, but also to draw attention to some of the unanswered questions. Everyone can help in the quest to unravel the story of Mendip's development and the people who lived and worked here in the past.

LOCAL AGENDA 21

Mendip District Council is committed to working with the local community in pursuing the aims and objectives of Local Agenda 21. This involves taking steps to improve the health and welfare of all people, ensuring that economic development takes place in a sustainable way, and safeguarding precious environmental assets.

The historic heritage is one of those non-renewable assets. The archaeological record contains scientific information about long-term human and environmental trends. A knowledge of the past helps to set our own society in context - today's communities did not arise in isolation, but are part of a continuum in which we can recognise ourselves as a living part of both the past and the future. There is a great deal of pleasure to be gained from our heritage; the buildings and character of our settlements and countryside are a source of delight and interest. Ecology and history are closely intertwined. All of Mendip's wildlife habitats are the result of past and present human management. For example, ancient lead-mining and quarrying has resulted in the development of areas of ecological importance. Even our most ancient woodlands have been shaped by many generations of management.

1 *Young people enjoying a mock excavation at the Peat Moors Visitor Centre.*

ABOUT THIS BOOK

Mendip District Council has published this book to help people to better understand and enjoy their historic heritage. It hopes to encourage Mendip's individuals and communities to take an active role in finding out about the history of their own settlements and landscapes, and to conserve the things that they value. The book aims to provide a meaningful and accessible introduction to the subject for people who may have little or no background knowledge. The huge range of the topic means, of course, that much information must be given in the form of generalisations, but these are enlivened and made relevant by detailed local examples. While a bibliography is included, here and there in the text are boxes drawing attention to especially interesting or helpful books or articles. Ideas for sites to visit and suggestions about how you can approach your own research projects are similarly highlighted.

In two appendices, readers can find information about the listed buildings and scheduled monuments in each parish. The vast majority of our historic sites and features fall outside these two protective designations, however, and information on them is held on the Sites and Monuments Register (SMR) that is maintained by Somerset County Council. This database is continually changing as new sites are discovered, but if you would like to know what is on the register for your parish, contact the SMR Officer for an up-to-date list. Mendip District Council also maintains a register of sites of historic interest, which is a little more wide-ranging than the SMR, and excerpts from the list are available on request. It is hoped that local people will add many more items to this list, and that they will enjoy the challenge of caring for their parish's historic treasures. In the course of researching this book, Mendip's communities were asked which aspects of their heritage they most valued; the replies were very varied and a selection is included in the appendix 'Things We Value'.

APPROACHES TO THE PAST

There are various approaches to finding out about the past. Sometimes a professional archaeological investigation is appropriate, usually when a site is threatened by development. More often our knowledge is increased by simply looking at maps and documents, and by walking in the countryside or round a settlement, looking and thinking about what we see. Anyone can join in the great adventure of discovering the history of their own area. Local people finding out about local places, investigating their own surroundings, and then taking steps to conserve places and features of interest is the essence of Local Agenda 21. Many groups and individuals are already enjoying exploring Mendip's historic heritage, but there is always more to be learnt - and new knowledge usually generates new questions.

A PAST WORTH PRESERVING

Mendip has a fine and exciting heritage of buildings, landscapes and buried archaeology. Every part of it is worthy of care, conservation and study. This does not mean fossilising the landscape, or living in the past. What it does mean is recognising the value of our heritage, understanding that each part of it is irreplaceable and not to be thrown away lightly. We already safeguard our best historic sites and buildings through scheduled monument and listed building controls, but many other buildings, countryside features and archaeological sites that are interesting and valuable are unprotected and often unrecognised.

A SHARED HERITAGE

Some of the story of Mendip's past has been recovered by professional historians and archaeologists, but much of it is the work of local people, unpaid enthusiasts and students. This book gathers together material that has been published in many books, papers and articles, and some that has not been published before, in an effort to share with a wider audience the excitement and delight of reaching a new understanding of our surroundings.

Mendip's special inheritance is in our stewardship. Only the people who live and work here can care for it. It belongs to us, but it also belongs to past and future communities, for the past becomes the present, and the present becomes the future in the twinkling of an eye. Mendip's past is a magnificent shared heritage whose future lies in our hands, a great privilege and a serious responsibility.

2 *Pump at Norton St Philip.*

CHAPTER 2

LIVING OFF THE LAND

For most of human history we have lived off the land by hunting, fishing and gathering. Farming is a relatively recent way of life. We have a background of more than a million years of survival by living in harmony with our surroundings, certainly exploiting natural resources, but probably not taking much part in shaping them.

The first evidence of early humans comes from Africa, and human groups probably did not reach Britain until about half a million years ago.

WESTBURY-SUB-MENDIP
Upper Palaeolithic
500,000 years before the present

Evidence from the quarry at Westbury-sub-Mendip suggests that Mendip was among the places visited by early humans. In 1969 a silted-up rock fissure was exposed high in the quarry face. In it were found a large number of fossilised animal bones. The animal remains were dated to about 500,000 years ago. The rift may have been the lair of bears or hyaenas, into which the bones of prey had been dragged. Among the bones were found the remains of jaguar, wolf, scimitar cat, bear, rhinoceros, horse and various small mammals. These species would have lived in a temperate climate. About 35 fragments of flint, some of which may have been roughly shaped into tools, were found in the rift, providing evidence of human activity in the cave.

THE ICE AGES
During the last 700,000 years, Britain has undergone 19 major climatic periods, half of which were warm and half cold. During both the warm and the cold periods there were episodes that were more temperate. Mendip was never covered by the ice sheets, but was very close to the southern edge of the glaciated area.

During the extremely cold periods, it was not possible for people to inhabit the area, but during warmer interludes there was some human activity here. Each time the ice sheets retreated northwards, a successional change in the environment took place. The sterile, frozen land surface gradually acquired grasses, ferns and hardy heathland shrubs. Mendip became a lichen-speckled tundra with patches of sedges and grassy areas surrounding lakes and bogs. Birch woods followed, giving way to pines, and finally broadleaf woodlands. Changes in flora were accompanied by changes in fauna.

Life in these very early and remote periods can be hard to imagine. *The Archaeology of Somerset* **by Mick Aston and Ian Burrow is a useful starting-point if you are keen to find out more.**

HYAENA DEN
Middle Palaeolithic

When you walk along the canal-side path leading from Wookey Hole Caves towards the paper mill, you pass a cave lying just across the canal. This is Hyaena Den. When workmen were cutting the canal in the 19th century, archaeological material was exposed in the entrance of the silted-up cave. The cave was first excavated by a local schoolboy, William Boyd Dawkins, who started work there in 1859, and later by the great Mendip caver and archaeologist H.E. Balch (also post master of Wells). Continuing investigations have found that human occupation of the cave took place about 34,000 years ago.

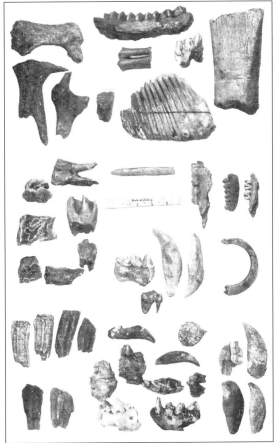

3 Teeth and jawbones from Hyaena Den.

The tools found in the cave are of a type associated with Neanderthal man, *homo sapiens neanderthalensis*. Neanderthals disappeared from the archaeological record and were replaced by *homo sapiens sapiens* (us) 30-40,000 years ago. We do not know how or why this happened, but we do know that there was human activity here in Mendip at the critical time. This means that the potential to answer fundamental questions about human development may be one of the most important aspects of Mendip's archaeology.

> **H.E. Balch was an intrepid and enthusiastic explorer of Mendip's caves. His wonderful archaeological collection can be seen in the museum he founded at Wells. His delightful little book *Mendip: The Great Cave of Wookey Hole,* first published in 1929, is a little outdated but still makes enjoyable reading.**

Hyaena Den has been interpreted as having two human occupation episodes, during which 11 small hand-axes were left behind. The cave was later used as a hyaenas' lair; among the many animal bones found in the cave were horse, hyaena, woolly rhinoceros, giant elk, and mammoth.

RETREAT OF THE ICE
Upper Palaeolithic, 10,000 - 8,500BC

The last ice sheet retreated about 10-12,000 years ago. As the climate warmed, the ecological succession began. The communities using the Mendip caves for shelter had access to a rich variety of plant and animal life. The upland area may have been a moss tundra with expanses of heather, bilberry, crowberry and some dwarf birch. In sheltered locations and on the lower ground, the land was probably more wooded, while the lower-lying areas supported grasses. Horse, red deer, smaller mammals and the brown bear were hunted. Some of Britain's most important archaeological sites of this early post-Ice Age period are in the Mendip Hills, mainly in the Cheddar Gorge area, but also near Wookey and in Burrington Combe.

> **Take a ramble in Ebbor Gorge, close to Wookey Hole, where the numerous little caves and rock shelters were used by humans and animals for thousands of years.**

NEW ENVIRONMENT NEW TECHNOLOGIES
Mesolithic, 8,500 - 4,500BC

As the climate warmed to a level approaching present-day averages, the environment changed to an ever-denser woodland cover. Hunting within this environment demanded different techniques from those appropriate to steppe-tundra conditions. The animals that were hunted also changed. Smaller, swifter animals were now the quarry. Changes in hunting techniques are evident from the new range of tools in use. Microliths - very small flint implements - are the characteristic tools of the Mesolithic culture. Larger flint implements - axes - were also used, probably for woodworking as well as for hunting and carcase preparation.

4 *Badger Hole may have been a seasonal camp in use for generations. It was found to contain many flint tools and animal bones and a fragment of a child's jawbone.*

Hunting bands may have become smaller, and the territories used by individual groups of people may have changed in size and type. Hunter-gatherers of this period were probably nomadic, moving around their territorial ranges to exploit varying resources at certain times of the year. Camp sites found in Mendip cover a range of landscape types, some high on the upland area such as Priddy and Badger Hole (near Wookey Hole), and others close to the low-lying wetlands, such as Godney ridge on the Somerset Levels.

A site of major importance close by is Gough's Cave at Cheddar, where thousands of flints and many animal bones were found. Horse formed a major part of the diet of these cave dwellers. Human bones were also found, with cut marks that may be evidence of cannibalism.

The skeleton of a hunter-gatherer found in Gough's Cave has recently been linked genetically by DNA testing to Adrian Targett, a history teacher at Kings of Wessex School. This amazing and exciting piece of research helps to make the past relevant to us all.

AN ISLAND IS BORN

Around 6,000BC, dramatic changes in sea level occurred, owing mainly to the large amounts of water involved in the freezing and thawing of the ice sheets. During the coldest periods vast quantities of water were locked in the glaciers overlying Europe and North America, and the shallower seas became dry. When the temperature warmed and the melt waters were released, the North Sea and the English Channel again separated Britain from the Continent.

Somerset had been separated from South Wales by low-lying plains until inundation created the Bristol Channel. Hunter-gatherer sites lie beneath the present sea, and the remains of Mesolithic camps and sub-merged forests can be seen at low tide in the inter-tidal zone along the coast of Somerset.

TIPPING THE ECO-BALANCE?

During this period some woodland clearance may have begun. Glades may have been created to encourage the browse for game, and to enable some wildlife management such as selective culling. Early woodland clearance may have permanently affected the eco-systems of marginal areas, tipping the balance between a wooded and an open environment. On Mendip this may have been the case in thin-soiled upland areas such as Blackdown.

Blackdown, above Charterhouse, is a marvellous place for a walk. The thin acid soils support little more than heather and bracken today, and may never have been very wooded.

5 *The bare heathland of Blackdown has been shaped by human activity over thousands of years.*

CHAPTER 3

EARLY FARMING SOCIETIES

THE FIRST FARMERS

Neolithic, 4,500 - 2,000BC

By about 7,000BC we can trace evidence of new human food-producing strategies in parts of southern Europe. A process of selection resulted in more productive cereal plants and domesticated animals. Farming slowly spread across Europe and first appeared in Britain by about 4,500BC. Other cultural changes seem to have arrived with agricultural techniques, notably production of the first pottery and the first recognisable ceremonial monuments. There must have been important changes to social structures and territories, but these are difficult to identify from the archaeological evidence.

*6 A Neolithic pot from
Tom Tivey's Hole, Leighton.*

The arrival of farming was the beginning of a more significant human influence on the Mendip landscape. Woodland clearance took place to make way for arable fields and pasture areas. Ground and polished flint axes and other stone axes of the period were used not only for clearance but also for woodland coppice management.

THE SWEET TRACK

Mendip's great contribution to knowledge of this period comes from the Somerset Levels and Moors, where researchers have investigated a series of ancient trackways and platforms preserved in the peat. Waterlogged peat provides exceptional conditions for the preservation of some types of organic matter. For over 20 years the peat moors have been the subject of an advanced programme of archaeological investigation and scientific analysis that has done much to further our knowledge of the development of the prehistoric environment.

Two important techniques used are environmental sampling and tree-ring dating (dendrochronology). Palaeoenvironmental sampling is the study of ancient environments from ecological evidence, such as pollen, seeds, and the remains of animals and insects. Dendrochronology is a technique for dating timber by observing patterns of thick and thin tree-rings and comparing them to a series of dated growth patterns. Trees grow strongly or weakly each year in response to differing climatic conditions. The pattern of good and bad growth years for trees has been analysed and used to create a time frame which reaches right back into prehistory.

7 A reconstruction of the Sweet Track, a Neolithic raised walkway through the marshes.

One trackway examined on the moors, the Sweet Track, is the earliest dated trackway in the world. It was named after Mr Sweet, the local farmer whose land it crossed. Dendrochronology has dated it to 3,807/6BC, making it nearly 6,000 years old. It was constructed of both coppiced wood and mature timber. The wood used included ash, oak, hazel, alder, holly, lime and elm. The heavy planks of oak, ash and lime were supported on a sophisticated arrangement of rails, poles and pegs.

The raised trackway provided a dry route across the marshes, joining two areas of higher ground, Shapwick on the Poldens to the south and the 'island' of Westhay to the north. It was over 1,500 metres in length. The trackway was in use for about 10 years, and then fell into disrepair, perhaps because of increasingly wet conditions in the marsh.

The Sweet Track was built and used by early farmers who were growing cereal crops and raising domesticated animals. Items dropped or deposited in the marsh alongside the trackway give us an insight into the lives of these people. There were pottery vessels, one containing hazelnuts and another with a wooden stirring-spoon. Wooden tools, flint knives, and some finely made arrowheads were also lost alongside the track. Some things may have been deliberately deposited in the marsh for ritual purposes; these include two unused axes, one of jadeite.

Although the Sweet Track has been lost in places, much of it survives beneath the peat. It is being conserved by a specially designed hydration system which prevents the timbers from drying out.

The Sweet Track is the oldest prehistoric trackway, but it is by no means the only example found in the levels. Others - of different design, materials and dates - have been uncovered. They all show that prehistoric people went to considerable trouble to exploit the resources of the wetland area, despite the difficulties of crossing the marshes.

Sweet Track to Glastonbury by J. Coles and B. Coles is a wonderfully readable book which gives a fascinating and informative insight into the trials and triumphs of archaeological research on the Somerset Levels.

THE GREAT MONUMENTS

The change from a hunting and gathering to a farming lifestyle was accompanied by another phenomenon. The landscape of Britain was altered by the creation of new ritual monuments. In Mendip we have several that date from this time.

Long Barrows

Long barrows in Britain vary in construction and form. There are two types recognisable locally: chambered tombs and earthen long barrows. Small clusters of long barrows existed on the central Mendip plateau and in the Frome area. The best surviving example is the chambered tomb that lies just outside the district at Stony Littleton.

Henge Monuments

Henges are enigmatic monuments, circular or oval enclosures usually enclosed by a bank with an internal ditch. They are presumed to have had ritual and ceremonial functions. Stonehenge is the most famous example of this class of monument, but its elaborate architecture seems to have been unique. Mendip's most impressive henge monuments, the Priddy Circles, consist of a set of three circular enclosures separated by a gap from a fourth incomplete one. A later Roman road runs through the gap. The three completed circles have diameters of 520 feet, the incomplete one, 560 feet. Visible in the banks, especially of the southernmost circle, are occasional very large stones, some of which are of silicified lower lias, the nearest known source of which is the deep depression called Wurt Pit about a mile away. A limited investigation of the southern circle showed that some upright stones were early features of the site. They had been replaced by a bank constructed of two concentric rings of posts, stakes and hurdles inside which stood two low drystone walls. Stone and earth were heaped on to this framework to form the bank.

8 *A Neolithic ground and polished flint axe found on the Somerset Levels.*

9 *Priddy Circles may be as old as the earliest phase of monument development at Stonehenge - much earlier than the famous arrangement of stones there today.*

Within a few miles of the Priddy group are a single henge monument at Gorsey Bigbury and two other possible henges, one near the Hunters Lodge Inn and another underlying the Roman amphitheatre at Charterhouse.

A WELL-EXPLOITED LANDSCAPE
Bronze Age, 2,000-650BC

The central plateau of Mendip continued to be a place of special significance in the Bronze Age. We can recognise from the archaeological evidence that cultural changes were taking place. The long barrows of the Neolithic period, large communal tombs, ceased to be built. Instead smaller, round burial mounds were constructed, reflecting a change in emphasis from the communal to the individual.

On the Mendip Hills there are more than 300 Bronze Age barrows. Some stand in isolation, others are in clusters and linear arrangements; they are of different sizes. The significance of the various sizes, sitings and arrangements is not yet understood.

Barrows can occur in lowland settings, but in Mendip most are in the upland areas. A concentration of barrows occurs on the central plateau, especially in the Priddy area. Another cluster lies to the north of Shepton Mallet, in Beacon Wood and the field to its west.

Beacon Wood was bought by Mendip District Council and gifted to the Woodland Trust to safeguard public access. You may wander freely around the woodland. See how many barrows you can find - some of them are easy to identify, but others are quite low mounds which are easily missed.

Many local barrows were excavated in the 19th century by the Reverend Skinner, a keen antiquary. Sadly, archaeological techniques of that date were woefully inadequate, so that much information which might have been recovered was lost.

The Reverend Skinner of Camerton, an energetic 19th century antiquarian, recorded his investigations in journals that are now in the British Library. They are very difficult to read because of his appalling handwriting, but they include many important early sketches and drawings of archaeological sites and landscapes. One of his journals has been published, and it is highly recommended for its colourful glimpses of Somerset village life. *Journal of a Somerset Rector, 1803-1834: John Skinner, A.M., Antiquary 1772-1839* edited by H. Coombs and A.M. Bax.

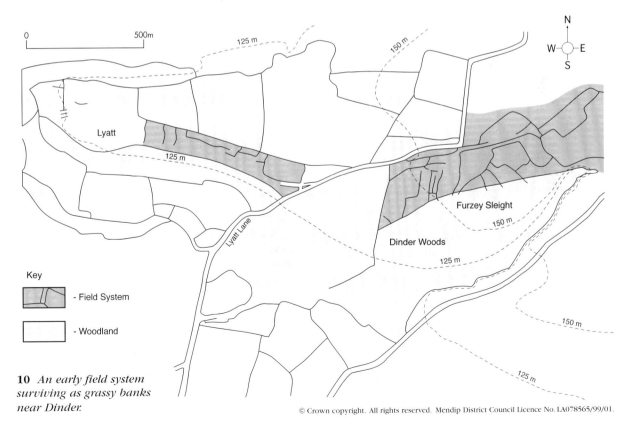

10 *An early field system surviving as grassy banks near Dinder.*

A few Bronze Age burials took place in Mendip caves. In a cave in Hope Valley, close to Ebbor Gorge, a skeleton with a gold bracelet was found; the bracelet was claimed by the landowner of the time and cannot now be traced.

The woodland clearance of much of Mendip probably took place during the Neolithic and Bronze Age periods, so that by about 1,000BC there was almost certainly considerably less woodland cover on the plateau than there is today. On Dartmoor and elsewhere, extensive field systems covering several miles were laid out at this time, showing that the landscape was widely exploited. There are a few surviving areas of early fields in Mendip. Although these fields were probably in use over a long period, they may have their origins in the Bronze Age. They are fairly regular arrangements of small square or rectangular units defined by banks and lynchets.

The banks and lynchets of early fields survive only where they have not been much disturbed by later activity, especially ploughing. This means that they are usually found on steep slopes, or on thin-soiled areas which were used exclusively as grassland in the Middle Ages and later.

To see ancient fields in Mendip, take the footpath that crosses the Lyatt and Furzy Sleight on the hilltop above Dinder. The small rectilinear fields here are a rare local survival, probably laid out in the prehistoric period.

Among the fields stood farmsteads and hamlets. Bronze Age farmsteads were round houses, with timber, wattle-and-daub or stone walls and thatched roofs - a style of housing that remained in use for many centuries. Houses were rebuilt every generation or so, often on the same site, but seem to have differed very little in design and construction over many centuries.

During this period the increasing appearance of weapons in the archaeological record speaks of growing social tension, perhaps because of pressure on resources from an increasing population. At the same time, we find defended enclosures being constructed. Above Westbury-sub-Mendip stands a large sub-circular enclosure which was probably created in this period.

11 *A reconstruction of a prehistoric roundhouse at the Peat Moors Visitor Centre, Westhay.*

CHAPTER 4

CELTIC CULTURE

IRON AGE

650BC-AD43

Aculture embraces many things: language, technology, religious belief, social structure, art, food and much more. Through the material evidence left behind we can recognise cultural changes that took place long ago. From about 650BC, changes in the archaeological evidence disclose new variations in some aspects of culture in Britain.

Art in particular was an area of change. Advances in technology, a high standard of craftsmanship, artistic achievement and appreciation speak of an intellectually sophisticated society with a love of beauty. Personal ornaments, pottery vessels, and other artefacts were different from those of the Bronze Age, while other aspects of material culture such as fieldscapes and building traditions changed little. It was once thought that the appearance of Celtic artefacts here indicated a folk invasion from the Continent, but now the view is that the indigenous communities of Britain, in common with communities over a wide swathe of Europe, incorporated Celtic cultural characteristics into their existing traditions.

Hillforts are wonderful places to visit. Not far from Mendip the country park at Ham Hill sits inside a huge Iron Age hillfort, and is a good place to experience the massive scale of the ditches and ramparts. Dolebury, just north of Shipham, belongs to the National Trust and is another fine site to explore. Within Mendip District, Maesbury Castle is a hillfort with a footpath running through the centre, giving walkers a chance to see its defences and enjoy the panoramic views.

HILLFORTS

The most exciting and prominent landscape legacy of the Iron Age must surely be the many hillforts that still dominate parts of the British countryside. They are among the most impressive of Mendip's archaeological sites.

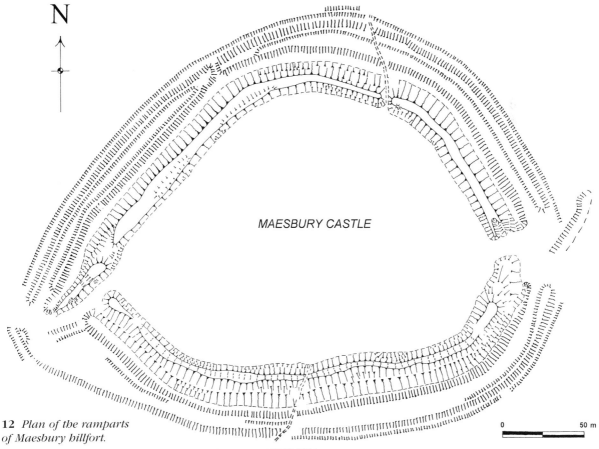

N

MAESBURY CASTLE

0   50 m

12 *Plan of the ramparts of Maesbury hillfort.*

Hillforts and hillslope enclosures fulfilled a number of different functions: some were proto-urban central places, others smaller defended settlements, with some perhaps serving as stock enclosures or seasonal camp sites. Not all of them were in contemporary use. It is likely that an early phase of a larger number of weakly defended enclosures gave way to a smaller number of more strongly defended successors. It is by no means certain that defence was always the major reason for the construction of elaborate ramparts; status and the outward display of communal effort may have been more important reasons for their construction.

A FRONTIER LAND

Society in the Iron Age was organised into tribal groups. Celtic culture was an heroic one in which fighting and cattle raiding were endemic, and we can assume that there was a degree of hostility and competition between neighbouring tribes. The tract of landscape which now makes up Mendip District straddles the boundary between the two great tribes of the Durotriges and the Dobunni. The Durotrigian lands stretched away to the south and east, with a major tribal centre at Maiden Castle near Dorchester, and important strongholds at Ham Hill and South Cadbury hillforts. The Dobunnic lands lay to the north, with their nucleus in Gloucestershire, and extending as far as Oxfordshire and Worcestershire. The political boundary between the two seems to have been the Brue Valley and the adjacent area of wetlands.

GLASTONBURY LAKE VILLAGE

During the late 1800s and early 1900s, an exciting excavation took place on the levels near Glastonbury. A local doctor, Arthur Bulleid, who was a keen amateur archaeologist, had read of prehistoric lake villages being found in Switzerland, France and Italy. Feeling sure that the marshes around Glastonbury would have the same sort of buried secret, he started to search for clues.

'On a Wednesday afternoon in March, 1892, when driving across the moor from Glastonbury to Godney, a field was noticed to be covered with small mounds, an unusual feature in a neighbourhood where the conformation of the land is for miles at a dead level. On the following Sunday afternoon the field was visited, and anticipations were agreeably realized by picking up from the numerous mole-hills

a number of pottery fragments, a whetstone, and pieces of bone and charcoal.'

He had discovered Glastonbury Lake Village. A man-made island of clay and timber (a structure called a crannog), with a landing-stage and palisade, had been constructed in a small area of fen carr surrounded by a shallow freshwater lake. The timber - mainly alder, willow and oak - was probably felled in the fen. Clay and rubble must have been brought from higher land by raft or boat, or perhaps in drier weather by mud sled. On the crannog, clay spreads had been laid to make floors, and round houses of timber, wattle and daub, and thatch had been constructed.

Because the site was waterlogged, the clay floors had to be renewed frequently by the addition of a fresh top layer of clay. Each time a new clay floor was spread, the hearth and any items that had been lying on the old floor were sealed between the two. In this way a fascinating layer-by-layer record of life on the site was built up. Even more importantly, the wet peat beneath and around the crannog preserved many organic objects - wooden artefacts, for example - which would not have survived on a dry-land site.

The artefacts found trapped in the clay floors, and other things that had been thrown into the water around the village, give us a vivid insight into the life of the people who lived there. They liked to wear jewellery; bracelets and finger rings made of Kimmeridge shale, and metal brooches were favourite items. They made textiles, spinning with spindle whorls, and weaving at looms. They were accomplished at metal-working and carpentry. They used pottery vessels, some quite plain, but others of beautiful form and design; this characteristically decorated pottery is known as Glastonbury-ware. Their diet was varied and nutritious, and included different types of cereals, beans, meat, fish, fowl, nuts, and fruit.

The lake village was founded in about 250BC. Something like eight generations of Iron Age folk lived there, with a population of between 100 and 200 inhabitants for over 200 years. It was a thriving, busy place which must have had a well-developed social life; the artefacts tell us unequivocally of an artistically sophisticated community with cultivated tastes and strong traditions.

13 *Iron Age Glastonbury-ware pottery drawn by Arthur Bulleid, a distinguished local amateur archaeologist who did much excellent research on the Somerset Levels in the late 19th and early 20th centuries.*

14 *Forestier's reconstruction drawing of the Glastonbury Lake Village. Recent re-interpretations of the evidence show that the crannog was much less crowded than this.*

It had been in decline for some 50 years before it was finally abandoned *circa* 50BC. We do not know why the site was deserted, but it seems likely that increasingly wet conditions made life progressively less comfortable in its last years of use.

An important recent study has re-interpreted earlier work on Glastonbury Lake Village. Coles and Minnitt's *Industrious and Fairly Civilized* is an essential book for anyone interested in the story of the Iron Age lake-dwellers.

Do visit the exceptional Glastonbury Lake Village Museum upstairs at The Tribunal, High Street, Glastonbury. This collection is of international importance, and is beautifully presented. The Glastonbury-ware pots are inspiring works of Celtic art, while the everyday objects of the long-lost settlement can be very moving. The lake village site is now a quiet field on the levels between Glastonbury and Godney; it belongs to the Glastonbury Antiquarian Society, as does the museum collection.

THE MEARE TRADING POSTS

Glastonbury Lake Village may have been the offshoot of an earlier bog settlement at Meare. Separated by about 100 metres of shallow water from the 'island' of Meare were two Iron Age settlements. These were constructed on the surface of a large raised bog where heather, sedge and moss clumps were interspersed with shallow puddles. The structures and shelters here were much more flimsy and temporary in nature than those of Glastonbury Lake Village. Settlement at Meare was probably seasonal, abandoned in the wetter months and rebuilt each summer.

The people were engaged in various handicrafts. Spinning, weaving and jewellery-making were important occupations; many objects of bone, horn and antler were used. Glass-making was an important activity at Meare. The glass beads made there were probably for necklaces, and perhaps also used to decorate clothing.

Meare's position on a tribal boundary, together with its impermanent nature, suggests that it was a seasonal trading post. Perhaps it was a place where exchanges both social and economic could safely take place in politically neutral territory.

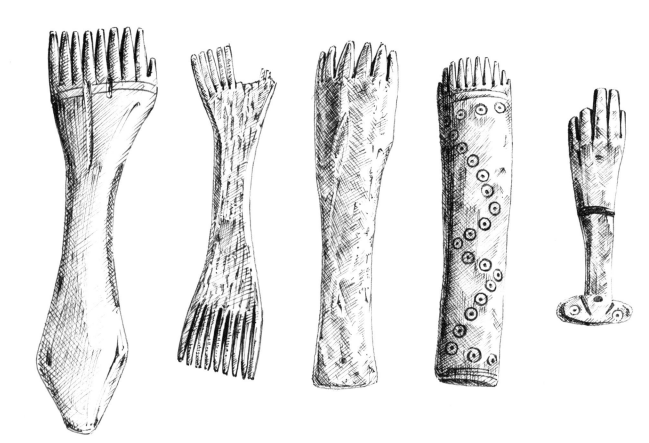

15 *Combs of bone or antler were used for textile working. One hundred and thirty weaving combs were found on the western settlement site at Meare.*

CHAPTER 5

THE ROMAN LEGACY

ROMAN

AD43-410

When we speak of Roman archaeology in Britain, we mean much more than the artefacts and structures made and used by foreign invaders. We mean also the artefacts and settlements of the native population during the period of the Roman occupation. Culture evolves, and during this period that of the local people changed to incorporate the use of Romanised styles in buildings, artefacts, technologies, and much more. So when we find Roman pottery in the plough soil, we do not think 'Romans were here', but rather 'People were here in the Roman period'.

Although the Roman interlude lasted for only about 350 years, its effect on the landscape and culture of Britain was enduring. Our Roman legacy has two aspects. Most obviously there was the direct imposition of military sites, new roads, towns, industrial works and so forth.

A more diffuse but equally significant creation was the evolution of a distinct Romano-British culture. The concept of Britannia, a province of the Roman Empire with a unified identity, was an important change. Previously there had been no sense of unity among the tribes, although strategic alliances may have been formed in times of war. During the Roman period, some sense of tribal identity remained and is recognisable in some aspects of the material culture, but it became secondary to the overarching concept of Britannia. Moreover, there was, at least at higher levels of society, a sense of belonging to the Roman Empire, so that an identifiable strand of Romanisation linked the people of Britannia with those of many far-flung lands. We may be sure that Latin was spoken and the toga worn by any wealthy person with social aspirations, whether they lived in Mendip, Macedonia or Mauretania.

There were many other cultural changes, both material and conceptual. A vastly increased range of manufactured goods became available, and they seem to have been within the reach of the whole population. Most settlement sites of the period have large quantities of pottery that was mass-produced in specialist areas of Britain, and smaller quantities of imported pots and wine jars are common.

Building design changed, and thatched round houses were replaced by rectangular ones, sometimes timber-framed but more often stone-built, with stone or ceramic roof tiles. Villas were built, some with considerable architectural sophistication, central-heating systems (hypocausts), mosaic floors and bath suites.

Take a walk up the quiet lane that runs north from Charlton, Shepton Mallet, to Beacon Hill. This is the Fosse Way, which ran from Devon to Lincoln. Like many Roman roads, its course has shifted slightly over the centuries, and here and there you can see the raised hump of the earlier road in fields to the west of the present lane.

ROMANS IN MENDIP

The Roman invasion of AD43 began in south-eastern England, but its effects were swiftly felt in the Mendip area. By AD49 the Romans were mining lead on Mendip, and the Fosse Way had been built. The Fosse Way served as a major strategic communications line. Beside the Fosse in Somerset were probably a number of forts - Bath, Camerton, Shepton Mallet and Ilchester are the likeliest places. Military evidence has been found at all but Shepton Mallet.

Although no fort has so far been found in Shepton Mallet, the evidence may yet be uncovered. There was certainly plenty of activity in the area of the present town. In the 19th century, Roman pottery kilns were found in the course of constructing the Anglo-Bavarian Brewery, and many burials were found in the adjacent area during other building work. More recently several excavations have taken place close to Fosse Lane, and a Romano-British village or small town has been partly uncovered.

ROMAN SHEPTON

We know rather little about most places in Mendip during the Roman period, but Shepton Mallet is an exciting exception. A series of investigations, beginning with the discovery of a lead coffin in 1988, have uncovered a fascinating lost settlement. Streets and enclosures, buildings and cemeteries, rubbish pits and industrial features all help us to build up a picture of life in the settlement. This seems to have been occupied by British people, who quickly adopted aspects of the Roman way of life.

16 *The Chi Rho amulet from Roman Shepton.*

17 *The Fosse Way at Shepton Mallet. The site of the 1990 excavations of the Romano-British settlement can be seen to the right of the road.*

Their buildings and pottery are instantly recognisable as belonging to the Roman period, but the decoration and form of some of their pottery owes much to earlier Celtic traditions.

Similarly, the burials found in the settlement reflect native as well as Roman customs. One grave at Fosse Lane contained a silver alloy amulet marked with a Chi Rho symbol. This is an early Christian symbol, formed by superimposing the Greek letters Chi (X) and Rho (R), the two first letters of the Greek word 'Christos'.

Roman Shepton functioned as a service and exchange centre for the locality. The inhabitants were engaged in farming and small-scale manufacturing, making tools, utensils (especially of pewter) and jewellery, perhaps supplying building materials, and providing a market for agricultural produce. On the south-western margin of the settlement, excavation uncovered building remains of the Bronze Age and Iron Age, so it seems likely that the Roman town developed from an established settlement. The evidence of timber buildings and burials cutting through the rubble of ruined Roman structures suggests that the settlement continued to be used into the Dark Ages.

Romans in Shepton Mallet: Excavations at Fosse Lane, 1990, published by Birmingham University Field Archaeology Unit, is an excellent booklet which contains lots of interesting information about the dig and photographs of the finds.

LAMYATT TEMPLE

One of the aspects of life that shows much continuity from the Iron Age to the Roman period is religion. In many cases similarities between Celtic and Roman gods were emphasised, so that British people continued to worship their old gods but under different names. Religion was a central theme of life in the Roman Empire, and there were many household and wayside shrines in addition to temples.

On the summit of Creech Hill at Lamyatt stood a Romano-Celtic temple. It was built in the 3rd century AD, of limestone, with hexagonal lias roofing slates. It had a plan typical of temples found throughout Gaul and Roman Germany. Locally a temple at Brean Down had a markedly similar plan, and both that site and Lamyatt were intervisible with a third temple at Cold Kitchen Hill, Wiltshire. There may have been close links between the three sites.

Both the Lamyatt and Brean Down temples seem to have been deliberately dismantled, and next to each was constructed a small single-cell stone building on an approximately east-west alignment. Close to each were a number of east-west burials. It is likely that these buildings were early Christian churches with cemeteries, successors to the Roman pagan temples.

A road leading to the Lamyatt temple left the Fosse Way on the top of Pennard Ridge. It is still a right of way in places, but much of the route has long since been abandoned. Lost sections of road can still be seen, especially where it has been terraced into the hillside. It was described as the 'miclan dic', the large dyke, in a Saxon document of AD955, when it served (as it still does) as a boundary between Ditcheat and Pennard.

A VIEW OF THE LANDSCAPE

The population of Roman Britain was high, perhaps between three and a half and five million. This was higher than ever before in the history of Britain, and was not to be paralleled until the 17th century. The landscape was fully utilised, with probably less woodland than exists in the modern countryside. The lowland landscape was covered with a network of small fields, many of which may have been laid out in the Bronze Age or Iron Age. Upland and wetland areas were probably largely unenclosed and used as rough pasture. Some drainage of the wetlands had taken place; Roman fields and farmsteads can be found in places that were too wet for such use in the Middle Ages. Settlements were mainly scattered farmsteads or small hamlets and villas. Small towns and market centres, such as Shepton, served local needs, while larger towns at Ilchester and Bath catered for a more sophisticated aristocratic market and functioned as administrative centres.

VILLA ESTATES

Few villas have been found in Mendip district. This is partly because little systematic fieldwork has been done, and partly because many of them may lie beneath today's settlements. It is probable that there was at least one villa in each of our parishes. Romano-British villa estates may have had their origins in pre-Roman arrangements. The villa estates may themselves have developed into medieval parish and hamlet territories.

THE LEAD INDUSTRY

The Romans were quick to exploit Mendip lead. They had long been mining it in Spain and elsewhere in the Empire; indeed, the lure of lead, silver and tin may have been one of the factors that encouraged the Emperor Claudius to proceed with the conquest. At Charterhouse a military fort was established, from which lead production was controlled. A settlement for workers was established, and an amphitheatre was built close by, possibly re-using an existing prehistoric field monument. To serve Charterhouse, a road was built leading eastwards towards Old Sarum and onwards towards the south-coast Roman port of Clausentum (Bitterne). The road is still in use in

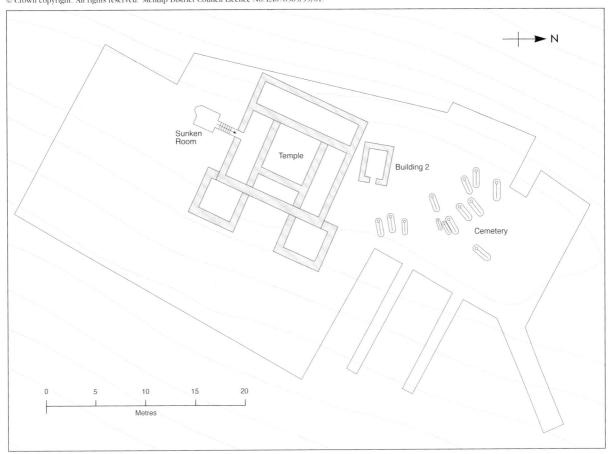

18 *Plan of the Romano-British temple, later building and cemetery at Lamyatt.*

places; elsewhere it can be traced here and there running through woods and fields, while other parts have been lost. The road may have continued to the west of Charterhouse, running along the Mendip plateau towards the natural harbour at Uphill.

While Charterhouse seems to have been the main centre of Roman lead-working, the industry was also active at other places in the area: at Priddy, East Harptree and Rookery Farm near Green Ore. The lead was smelted and formed into large ingots or pigs, and small quantities of silver were probably extracted. Lead was used for plumbing and for coffins, sheets of it lined the great bath at Aquae Sulis (Roman Bath), and it was added to tin to make pewter. Pewter tableware was made at several sites in north Somerset, including Shepton Mallet. Mendip lead has been found far from Somerset, in Rome itself, and beneath the ashes of Pompeii.

20 *At Lower Whatley a large and sophisticated villa has been partly excavated, and a fine mosaic floor uncovered. Sadly, the mosaic was left open to view beneath a specially built shelter, and was gradually destroyed by theft.*

19 *Pewter vessels of the Roman period.*

Charterhouse, in the heart of the Mendip plateau, is a wonderful place to visit. From the steep hill called Rains Batch you can look down on the remains of the Roman fort, while close by in Blackmoor Reserve you can wander among the deep rakes that were dug to extract lead nearly 2,000 years ago. The Charterhouse Centre organises a variety of outdoor activities, including guided walks, and there are leaflets available for visitors who prefer to explore on their own.

A light-hearted read, which gives a flavour of the past, is the novel *The Silver Pigs* by Lindsey Davis. It is partly set in Charterhouse during the Roman period.

21 *Students from Exeter University excavating at Charterhouse. Roman pottery was found in this rake or lead-mine.*

CHAPTER 6

THE MISTS OF TIME

DARK AGE & EARLY MEDIEVAL

AD410-1066

Our understanding of the end of Britain's phase as a province of the Roman Empire is hazy. Certainly the Empire was under pressure from barbarians. We know from the classical sources that from the 360s Britannia had been struggling against raiding Picts, Scots and Saxons. The classical writer Zosimus tells us that in 410 the Emperor Honorius replied to an appeal for help from Britannia by telling the cities to look after their own defence. Thereafter there seems to have been no Roman military presence here.

The mysterious, turbulent post-Roman years are often called the Dark Ages. It is to this period that the legends of King Arthur belong; the story is a vivid symbol of the Romano-Celtic struggle against Anglo-Saxon raiders. The invaders gained increasing areas of territory, initially in the south-east. They probably seized control of Somerset in AD658, after a battle which the *Anglo-Saxon Chronicle* tells us happened at Peonnum (perhaps Penselwood). Somerset became part of the large Saxon kingdom of Wessex.

With the withdrawal of Rome had come economic collapse. Organised industries ceased as markets disappeared. We can see that many Romano-British settlements were abandoned or reduced in size and status at some time between the 5th and 10th centuries. It seems certain that there was a considerable drop in population, which may have halved or worse.

The *Anglo-Saxon Chronicle* records many battles against Danish invaders in the 9th and 10th centuries. No direct evidence of Viking raids has yet been found in the Mendip area, but the monastery at Glastonbury would have been a tempting target for plunderers, and it may have been badly affected.

The archaeological evidence for this period is difficult. Coins and pottery provide much of the datable evidence for archaeologists, but for 500 years after the end of Roman Britain both were scarce in Somerset. This paucity of evidence means that very few sites of the period have been recognised and examined. In Mendip we have one of the most dramatic Dark Age sites in Britain, Glastonbury Tor.

Glastonbury Tor belongs to the National Trust. Large numbers of visitors climb the Tor each year, mainly for the glorious views of Glastonbury, the Somerset Levels and the Mendip Hills. Such visitor pressure causes damage, but taking care to remain on the surfaced path will help to minimise erosion.

GLASTONBURY TOR

The summit and shoulder of Glastonbury Tor were excavated in 1964-6. Erosion and levelling of the site for the medieval church, together with the naturally fissured nature of the bedrock on the exposed hilltop, made this a difficult site to interpret. Flints and a stone axe showed that the site had at least been visited in prehistoric times. A small amount of Roman pottery and tile was found, although this may have been brought to the site in the Dark Age occupation phase.

22 *Glastonbury Tor - an enigmatic Dark Age settlement site.*

The excavations showed that the Tor had been an occupation site in the 5th to 7th centuries. Sherds of imported Mediterranean pottery were found, the remains of amphorae which had contained wine, olive oil or other exotic imports. Similar pottery has been found at South Cadbury Castle, Cannington, Cadbury-Congresbury, Tintagel and other apparently high-status sites of the period. Many animal bones were found on the Tor, the remains of joints of meat that had been butchered elsewhere. The post-holes of timber buildings, hearths, pits and evidence of metal-working were uncovered.

Enigmatically, two graves lay orientated south-north. In most circumstances we would expect Christian graves to lie west-east, although these two were perhaps affected by the extremely constricted conditions of the summit, and may have made use of existing fissures in the rock. Interestingly, there was a medieval tradition of an early monastery on the Tor, with two hermit monks named Arnulph and Ogmar.

The Tor was a special place in the Dark Ages, with a small number of people living on the exposed and inhospitable summit and having access to imported goods from the Mediterranean. This may be interpreted as making it either the highly defendable eyrie of a warrior chieftain, or an early monastery. The known existence of the 10th century monastery of 'St Michael on the Tor' suggests that the latter is the more likely, particularly in view of Glastonbury's later importance as a monastic centre.

GLASTONBURY ABBEY

Glastonbury Abbey is sometimes called 'the cradle of Christianity'. A history of the abbey compiled by William of Malmesbury in the 12th century claimed that the small wattle church which was the earliest church on the site was the most ancient in Britain, built by missionaries sent from Rome in the second century AD. Despite archaeological investigation of the site over the past 90 years, no evidence has yet been found to confirm this alleged early origin. Indeed, the evidence from the Tor is earlier than that forthcoming so far from the abbey site.

Traditionally Glastonbury Abbey was associated with a number of Celtic saints - St Patrick, St Collen and St Bridget - and it had a number of small, outlying churches in isolated marshland settings at Beckery, Street, Marchey, Nyland, Godney and Meare. These isolated churches may have their origins in the hermitages of the Celtic tradition. The chapel at Street was called Llantokay, which means 'the holy enclosure of St Kay', and was clearly an early site with Celtic Christian associations. The monastery at Glastonbury was certainly founded by AD700 at the latest, when the West Saxon

23 *St Aldhelm's Well, Doulting.*

King Ine built a church at Glastonbury. There was a church on the present site by the 10th century.

Viking raids may have severely damaged or destroyed the monastery during the 9th century. William of Malmesbury recorded that there had been no monks at Glastonbury from the time of King Alfred until the mid-10th century, although it was still occupied, possibly by Irish clerics. It was revived by St Dunstan, who was appointed abbot and granted royal permission to refound Glastonbury in about 940. By the time of the great 11th century survey, the *Domesday Book*, Glastonbury had become the richest monastery in England, with extensive and productive estates to support its community and fund its building works.

There are two unusual and important archaeological features associated with Glastonbury but lying outside the town. The first, Ponters Ball, is an impressive and enigmatic linear earthwork which lies on either side of the main Glastonbury to Shepton Mallet road close to Havyatt. Up to 10 metres wide and 3.5 metres high, it runs for more than a kilometre between low-lying areas across the strip of higher land by which Glastonbury is approached from the east. Ponters Ball is at present undated, but seems most likely to be prehistoric, Dark Age or early medieval.

The second feature is a Saxon watercourse that ran for over a mile between Northover and the centre of Glastonbury. It is still visible in places at the foot of Wearyall Hill. This waterway has been interpreted as a Saxon canal, perhaps providing a ceremonial approach to the abbey. It may be the work of St Dunstan.

You can see the course of the ancient canal alongside the road from Glastonbury to Street at the foot of Wearyall Hill. It has been investigated by archaeologists Charles and Nancy Hollinrake, who in 1992 published an account of their research in the *Proceedings of the Somerset Archaeological and Natural History Society*, vol. 136, pp.73-94.

OTHER EARLY CHRISTIAN SITES

Mendip has an exceptional heritage of places with early Christian associations. At Wells the development of the Saxon cathedral on the site of a late Roman mausoleum suggests a continuity of spiritual importance from the Roman period to the present day. There was a late Roman Christian community at Shepton Mallet, and it seems likely that the early church close by at Doulting was that community's successor. A minster church was founded at Doulting by St Aldhelm in the 7th century, and this foundation may have represented the bringing of an ancient Celtic foundation into the establishment of the Roman Church.

You will find St Aldhelm's Well standing beside a quiet lane close to Doulting Church, where the clear waters of the spring gush from the hillside into a stone trough.

The minster church at Frome was also a foundation of St Aldhelm's. Minsters were religious houses with a mission to spread Christianity to the people living in their *parochiae* or territories. Each royal estate probably had a minster. The very large parish of St Cuthbert Out in the Wells area may be a rare survival of a Saxon *parochia*, an early ecclesiastical territory. Most of these large territories were later divided into smaller parishes, but for some reason St Cuthbert Out was never subdivided. Other churches in the area with evidence of early origins are East Pennard, Kilmersdon and Chewton Mendip, all probable minsters.

24 *There has been a church at East Pennard since at least 955.*

CHARTERS AND PLACE-NAMES

While archaeological evidence for the 500 years from the end of Roman Britain is scanty, documents and place-names are important sources of information for the Saxon period. Charters recorded grants of land and often ended with a clause describing the bounds of the granted territory. The features mentioned in the boundary clauses can often be identified from surviving landscape features such as roads and streams, while field names and minor place-names can help to solve other parts of the puzzle.

Place-names are full of meaning, and can help us to build up a picture of the landscape in the 7th to 11th centuries. Clusters of place-names including Saxon woodland elements such as 'leah', 'wudu', 'bearu', 'graf', 'hyrst' and 'holt' show areas of well-wooded landscape, while their absence demonstrates countryside with little tree cover.

From the woodland elements in place-names, try picking out areas that were well wooded in the past. Larger woodland areas can be discovered from looking at clusters of village and hamlet names, while smaller lost woods can be identified from old field names.

The way in which large estates functioned can be partly illuminated by place-names. A cluster of place-names incorporating Saxon personal names plus 'ington' surrounding the large royal estate of Frome shows places that were granted by Saxon kings to minor lords: Beckington, Lullington, Hardington, Hemington, Tytherington, etc. Names that have been derived from estate functions are Buckland (bookland - land granted out by charter), Faulkland (folkland - land held by the king that could be granted for life but not permanently disposed of), Walton (estate of the slaves or Welsh), and Charlton (estate of the ceorls, free royal servants).

If you would like to learn more about Saxon Somerset, Dr Michael Costen's book *The Origins of Somerset* is highly recommended.

SETTLEMENT AND COUNTRYSIDE

This turbulent half millennium saw some important changes in the human geography of the landscape. Many Romano-British settlements were abandoned, but many others continued in use and probably lie beneath the farmsteads, hamlets and villages of the modern landscape.

In some places, new villages and hamlets were planned and founded, often accompanied by new agricultural arrangements. Areas for arable cultivation were divided into large fields, often two or three, of which one would be left fallow and available for grazing each year. Each field consisted of subdivisions - furlongs - which themselves were divided into long, narrow strips. The cultivators' landholdings typically consisted of a number of strips dispersed among the furlongs and fields of the community. Other landscape resources such as woodland, rough pasture and meadow were often held in common. Arrangements such as this, known as open-field or common-field systems, were once thought to have been introduced in the early Saxon period, but research now suggests that they may date from a century or so before the Norman Conquest.

Just outside Mendip, at Shapwick, a multi-disciplinary project is under way to examine the origins of the village and its fields. The findings are published in *The Shapwick Project Annual Reports* available through the library service or from the Centre for Historic Environment, Dept of Archaeology, University of Bristol.

25 *Fieldwalking, the systematic collection of archeological evidence from plough soil, cannot help us to identify Dark Age and Early Medieval sites, as there was virtually no pottery in use in Somerset at this time.*

CHAPTER 7

MEDIEVAL MENDIP

THE MIDDLE AGES
1066-1540

By the middle of the 13th century, much of the character of Mendip as we now know it had been formed. All of the larger settlements and many of the hamlets and farmsteads of the modern landscape were already in existence. Much of the present-day network of highways and tracks had been established. There have been many changes of detail - in the size of settlements and in the arrangement of agricultural plots - but the most notable and extensive differences between the modern and medieval landscapes of Mendip are to be found in the enclosure and improvement of the low-lying wetlands and the upland pastures.

During the Middle Ages, the wetlands - which were known as the moors - were used as seasonal pasture by communities living on their margins. There were extensive open tracts of rough, upland pasture on the Mendip plateau, which had fewer settlements than today, since many of the modern farmsteads post-date the Parliamentary Enclosures of the 18th and 19th centuries. The plateau was by no means without settlement, however: there were a number of upland farms, most of them held by the church. Green Ore (then Greenworth), for instance, was held by the monks of Hinton Charterhouse, and another local Carthusian monastery, Witham, held land at Charterhouse-on-Mendip. The Knights Templar held Temple Hidon close by, and Ellick above Burrington Combe belonged to St Augustine's Priory, Bristol.

The settlements adjacent to the central Mendip area each had rights of pasture on the unenclosed uplands, and the area was also used for lead-mining and other mineral extraction. That its greatest value was in its pastoral resources rather than mineral wealth is clear from the accounts of the Bishop of Wells's estate in 1310, when the profits from lead were little over a pound, while those from summer pasture were more than 43 pounds.

ESTATES

Lordly landholders had immense influence over the shaping of the medieval landscape. The church held vast tracts of land, with Glastonbury Abbey, the wealthiest monastery in England at the Norman Conquest, by far the biggest landholder locally. The church and crown between them controlled 76% of Mendip. To provide for their needs, they managed their landholdings in a variety of ways. Some manors were directly farmed, others were granted to nobles in exchange for knightly service, still others were rented out, or allotted to the providers of special services.

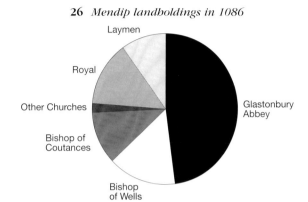

26 *Mendip landholdings in 1086*

Markets and towns were developed, providing outlets for farming products, centres for craftwork, and easily won income in the form of rents, tolls and taxes for their lords. Manor houses, sometimes moated, nestled beside churches, mills were built, parks created, fish-ponds dug, farm buildings constructed.

Find out about your own parish in the 11th century by looking up its entry in the *Domesday Book*. This great survey was undertaken for William the Conqueror, to give him information about the wealth of the country and to show what estates were held by the crown, by the church, and by great and lesser lords. The landscape information in the book is enigmatic but fascinating. A good edition is *Domesday Book Somerset* by Caroline and Frank Thorn.

The power and resources of the large ecclesiastical lords made possible large-scale water engineering works. Glastonbury Abbey, for example, undertook extensive work on the course of the River Brue. It was channelled and re-routed by 200 metres or more between Baltonsborough and Glastonbury, while to the west of the town a completely new river course was cut, taking it through Meare instead of through the Panborough Gap to the north. On the lands of the Bishop of Wells there were also major alterations to the watercourses. The streams flowing through Wells were harnessed to supply the palace moat and water for the townspeople, and to power the mills of the town. A millstream was engineered to take water from the Axe for miles along the foot of the Mendip slopes through Wookey, Henton, Bleadney and Panborough.

FORESTS AND PARKS

Among the luxuries of medieval lords were lands dedicated to the pleasures of the chase. Forests were areas designated by the king as being subject to special jurisdiction, forest law. Within the forest there were stringent restrictions aimed at protecting game. The word 'forest' comes from a Norman French term meaning 'the land without' - without, or outside, common law. Forests were sometimes, but not always, wooded areas. In Mendip there were two royal forests, Selwood and Mendip. They were very different in character. Selwood was well wooded. Its earlier (Celtic) name was *Coit Maur*, the Great Wood; it had been a landscape boundary of major political importance from at least the early Saxon period, and perhaps long before. It was a great royal hunting ground, which extended in a strip two to five miles wide along the greensand ridge. The bounds of the forest were described in a number of documents, and many of them can be matched to the modern landscape.

The Forest of Mendip was not wooded, but mainly open, heathy countryside, similar to the forests of Exmoor and Dartmoor. It may have been a more extensive hunting preserve in the Saxon period, but in the High Middle Ages it consisted mainly of the Cheddar and Charterhouse area, and measured about three miles north to south and four miles east to west. It was effectively abolished as a hunting forest in 1338, but the term remained in use to describe the open, common pastures of Mendip until the enclosures of the 18th and 19th centuries.

Deer parks abounded in the area during the Middle Ages. They were used for raising and hunting deer, but were also part of the vital landscape resources of woodland and pasture. For example, Glastonbury Abbey's great park at Pilton, approximately a square mile in area, was not solely devoted to deer. It supplied twelve oak trees for building a new sheep house at Mells in the early 14th century, and some local tenants had the right to graze sheep and oxen there. The tenants of other manors of Glastonbury Abbey's great estate had a duty to 'enclose the park of Pilton' every year, each manor being required to keep a specified length of the park boundary in good repair.

Larger parks sometimes contained lodges or hunting boxes, and rabbit warrens and fishponds were commonly found. Medieval deer parks in Mendip include those of the abbots of Glastonbury at Wirral, Norwood, Pilton and Sharpham, those of the bishops of Wells at Wells, Westbury-Sub-Mendip, and Evercreech, and those of other lords at Chewton Wood, Downhead, Farleigh Hungerford, Lydford, and Hardington.

CHURCHES

The churches of Mendip are among its chief glories, each of them bearing witness to the passing generations; to the communities who built them, re-shaped them to meet changing needs, worshipped in them, and marked the passing of seasons and of lifetimes through their rites and monuments. The 15th century towers of Somerset churches are among the finest in England, and were built from the profits of the woollen cloth industry. Churches such as Leigh-on-Mendip and Batcombe express the prosperity and creative exuberance of the later Middle Ages.

The story of a settlement is contained partly within its church architecture. Places that had large and wealthy communities in the Middle Ages have bequeathed us fine and spacious churches such as Mells. Smaller and poorer medieval communities have handed down more modest churches. Where the church stood close to a lord's favoured residence, its grandeur may reflect the wealth of the lord rather than that of his tenants.

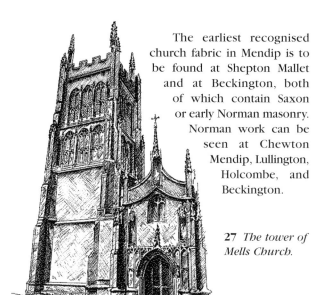

The earliest recognised church fabric in Mendip is to be found at Shepton Mallet and at Beckington, both of which contain Saxon or early Norman masonry. Norman work can be seen at Chewton Mendip, Lullington, Holcombe, and Beckington.

27 *The tower of Mells Church.*

28 *The Norman doorway of Lullington Church.*

Your local church is a wonderful resource for historical research. Most of them have been altered and partially rebuilt over the centuries, and now contain a patchwork of architectural features from different periods. Try working out how old the various features of your church are with the aid of a handbook on church architecture. Two very useful booklets are *Churches and Chapels: Investigating Places of Worship* and *Recording a Church: An Illustrated Glossary,* both published by the Council for British Archaeology.

RURAL MONASTERIES AND GRANGES

In addition to the urban ecclesiastical houses of Wells, Glastonbury and Frome, there were a number of rural monasteries, granges and hospitals in Mendip.

Witham Friary

Witham Priory, the first Carthusian monastery in Britain, was founded in the late 12th century as part of Henry II's atonement for the death of Thomas à Becket. The archaeology of Witham Priory reflects the hermit-like character of the order. The monastery was situated at some distance from the present village, which was the site of the lay brothers' accommodation. The name Witham Friary is derived from the French word for brother, *'frère'*; the *'frerie'* was the place where the lay brothers lived.

Major earthworks survive inside the monastic enclosure and, close by, the priory fishponds are still fished. In the village itself there remain two medieval buildings, a 14th century dovecote and the church. The church may contain earlier work; it has been suggested that the rough masonry visible in the window arches belongs to a Saxon church that has been encased in the thick 12th century walls. The font dates from just after the Black Death. Before the great plague the labour for running the estate was provided by celibate lay brothers, but afterwards, difficulty in recruitment led to the employment of married men, bringing families to the village for the first time in a century and a half.

29 *The monastic fishpond that lies beside the site of Witham Priory is still fished today.*

The high pastures of Charterhouse on Mendip belonged to the monks of Witham Priory, from which association it draws its name. The word 'charterhouse' was derived from the mother house of the Carthusian order, *La Grande Chartreuse* near Grenoble, France. Charterhouse was a detached part of the parish of Witham Friary until the l9th century. A grange (farm) belonging to the priory was probably situated on the site of the present Lower Farm.

Witham Church is a fascinating place to visit; it has been altered several times, but still retains something of a French character, the legacy of 12th century monks from the Alps. A very good book about the priories at Witham and Hinton is *The Somerset Carthusians* by Margaret Thompson.

Hinton Charterhouse Priory, which lies just outside Mendip, close to Norton St Philip, was the second English Carthusian house, founded by Countess Ela of Salisbury, who in a single day founded the nunnery at Lacock and the monastery at Hinton. The priory had a grange at Green Ore, then called Greenworth. Green Ore, like Charterhouse, was free from tithes and taxes because of a special dispensation granted to the monastery, and still retained its special extra-parochial status 600 years later when the tithe map for the surrounding parish of Chewton Mendip was drawn up. Hinton Charterhouse had other lands in Mendip, including a lease on Lechmere Water, Emborough.

Norton St Philip

As part of its foundation grant, Hinton Priory was given the adjacent manor of Norton St Philip. It seems likely that the monastery tried to develop Norton as a new town during the 14th century. The priory was under financial pressure at that time, and may have hoped that the rents, taxes and market tolls from a town would rescue their fortunes. The George, a magnificent 14th century inn, must have represented a considerable investment, but it would have been an important asset of the embryonic town. It accommodated merchants and other traders, and provided storage facilities for wool and cloth to be sold in the market-place in front of the inn.

30 The George Inn, Norton St Philip, may have been built by the monks of Hinton Priory as part of a new town foundation in the 14th century.

A visit to the George at Norton St Philip is highly recommended. It is one of the finest remaining medieval inns in England.

A little way from the George, in the Manor Farm area, was a grange complex. A grange was an outlying farm belonging to a religious house. This is a rare survival, with much medieval fabric remaining in a relatively unchanged setting. The grange was set inside a large walled enclosure, which still exists. The manor house, altered in the 17th and 18th centuries, was originally a high-status eight-bay building of the 14th century. A medieval barn and dovecote survive, and the remains of a gatehouse form part of a cottage that stands beside the entrance to the former enclosure. Further buildings in the immediate area may have medieval origins, including one that may have been a chapel to the grange complex.

Glastonbury Abbey had granges at some of their manors. Surviving Glastonbury manor houses in Mendip are at Norwood, Walton, Ivythorn, Sharpham, and Meare. At Pilton, Ditcheat and Mells, some medieval fabric may have survived later rebuildings. Fine barns belonging to the abbey survive at West Bradley, Pilton, Doulting, Mells and Glastonbury.

The manor house at Meare stands in a wonderfully unspoilt setting beside the church and Fish House. All three are 14th century buildings. A medieval wall survives behind the manor house, probably the remains of a medieval garden. Abbot Bere enlarged an earlier small garden or pleasaunce at Meare by walling in more than three acres and making moats, pools and orchards. The Fish House, with its complex of ponds for fish farming, lay beside a great freshwater lake known as Meare Pool. Five miles in circumference, it provided fish, eels and waterfowl for the monastery. Meare Pool was drained in the 17th century as part of the reclamation of the wetlands, but it can sometimes be seen again when the moors flood and a great sheet of shining water, half a mile in diameter, once again lies between Meare and Godney.

At Wookey there was a palace for the Bishop of Wells. Some of the fabric survives in the building of the present Court Farm.

Adjacent to the house is an extensive area of earthworks. At Evercreech the bishops had a favourite manor house and a deer park. The location of the manor house is not known, but it may have been on the site of the present Park Farm.

At Beckington the medieval building of Beckington Abbey and The Grange (two separate properties, but a single building) may have housed a hospital of Augustinian canons. Two other religious houses had property at Beckington. The priors of Maiden Bradley were lords of the manor of Beckington Priors during the Middle Ages. Court rolls attest the presence of a grange here, probably situated at Prior's Court Farm. The Prior of Longleat held a tenement in Beckington and court rolls show that here, too, were substantial stone-built grange buildings: the site of these buildings is not known.

A small monastery, Langley, existed near Frome, probably on or near the site of St Algar's Farm. Also in Mendip lay several properties belonging to the Knights Templars and the Knights Hospitallers. Temple Hidon, close to Charterhouse on the Mendip plateau, is among the best known, but at Coleford the establishment known as Temple Newbury was probably situated at or very near the present Page House Farm.

RURAL LIFE

There were acute demographic swings during the Middle Ages. Between the late 11th century and the early 14th, there was a huge increase in population, which may even have doubled. As a result, more and more land was pressed into use for growing crops. Steep hillsides that had long been used as pasture land were ploughed, woodlands were completely felled or nibbled into in the clearance process called 'assarting'. This intensive cultivation period has left us a fascinating legacy of landscape features - the ridge and furrow of strips ploughed long ago by teams of oxen, the grassy terraces on hillsides which are strip lynchets, where once land-hungry farmers scraped a livelihood from unsuitable terrain.

The whole landscape was exploited under the control of the manorial lords - woodland and meadow, arable land and rough pasture, all were subject to regulation. This has left us with a wonderful legacy of medieval documents, surveys, accounts and court records, which tell us in detail about aspects of the life of ordinary farmers and cottagers. The Glastonbury Abbey documents have survived particularly well, many having been acquired by the Thynne family after the Dissolution under Henry VIII and preserved at Longleat House. A fine collection of medieval documents pertaining to Wells has also survived.

31 *The long, narrow fields at Withial, East Pennard, were enclosed in the early 17th century, preserving the pattern of medieval arable strips. The ridge and furrow formed by ploughteams of oxen can still be seen in places.*

If your parish belonged to either Glastonbury Abbey or Wells Cathedral during the Middle Ages, you will probably be able to find some printed transcriptions of medieval documents for your area - although they may be in Latin. Street Library has volumes for the Glastonbury Abbey estate, and Wells Library has volumes for Wells Cathedral's possessions. Check in the *Local Studies Parish Pack* at your nearest public library to find out who owned your parish in the past.

Peasant landholdings were small. There was an established system of tenement holdings, which varied somewhat from estate to estate, and from region to region. On the Glastonbury Abbey estate, peasants were classed, according to the size of their land holdings, as virgators, half virgators, ferdellars (with a quarter of a virgate), and cottars (with almost no land). Virgates on the estate were probably made up of 40 arable acres, with rights to grazing, hay meadow, and woodland according to an agreed livestock rate. As most Glastonbury Abbey manors operated a two-field cultivation system, the tenants could grow crops on only half of their holdings each year, the other half lying open for common grazing. The crops grown were mainly wheat and oats supplemented with small amounts of rye, barley, beans and some obscure crops and mixed cereals called drowa, drage and mixtillo.

The growing population needed not only land but homes. Some settlements expanded haphazardly, resulting in a confused, agglomerated settlement plan. Others were planned and set out in a regular form.

By the mid-14th century the population level was in sharp decline, hastened but not precipitated by the coming of plague, the dreadful Black Death. The population was already weakened before the arrival of the plague, which followed a series of famines caused by disastrous harvests resulting from wet summers. There were probably no villages in Mendip that failed completely due to the plague, but many settlements were weakened. The humps and bumps of former house sites can be found in many villages and hamlets. In the longer term, some settlements went out of use altogether, and there may be a few farmsteads and small hamlets in Mendip that never recovered from the Black Death.

The humps and bumps of the deserted medieval hamlet of Ramspits can be visited at the Deerleap Reserve about a mile to the north-west of Wookey Hole. Before you go, read the article about the site in the *Proceedings of the Somerset Archaeological and Natural History Society*, vol. 135.

THE TOWNS

There were four medieval towns in Mendip: Wells, Glastonbury, Frome and Shepton Mallet. Of these, the first three developed around important ecclesiastical centres. Each of these major churches would have attracted service providers and traders, and so settlements must soon have grown up in their vicinities. Their development into towns may have been a gradual process or may have resulted from deliberate foundation policies.

Frome

The monastery of St John was established in the 7th century by St Aldhelm, close to the great wooded hunting preserve of Selwood. It has been suggested that the monastery was established within the great wood, but it is perhaps more likely that Frome was established in long-cleared land to the west of the wood. This provides a more convincing context for known prehistoric and Roman sites in the area, such as the long barrows at Fromefield House and Murtry, and the Roman settlement near Orchardleigh.

32 *Medieval Cheap Street, Frome.*

During the Saxon period, Frome was the centre of a large royal estate. There are records of visits by Saxon kings at various dates, and an important meeting of statesmen and nobles - a witangemot - was held there in 934. It is thought that in 955 King Eadred died at Frome, and it is very likely that there was a royal palace in the area. At Cheddar the Saxon palace lay some distance from its town of Axbridge, and it may be that a palace associated with Frome lies outside the town, perhaps at Vallis, the manorial centre of the main Frome estate, which was held from the king in the 12th century by the powerful Norman Courcelles family.

By the time of *Domesday Book* (1086), Frome had a valuable market, and throughout the Middle Ages it was a thriving market town, with an economy founded firmly on the woollen cloth trade. The course of the River Frome was altered to optimise its use for powering fulling and corn mills. Its present course to the east of the bridge was formerly that of the mill leat.

The town sat within a very large parish, and was closely integrated with the surrounding countryside. Townsfolk traded and manufactured, but they also farmed the land. Cirencester Abbey was granted the minster lands in the 12th century and managed them until the dissolution of the monastery.

Much of Frome's medieval heritage is contained within its steep and winding street pattern, and its surviving early buildings. The remains of the chantry chapel of St Catherine may be contained in buildings at Catherine Hill.

Do visit Frome Museum, which has a lovely model of the town on display and many exhibits relating to the town's rich history. It also has an excellent small bookshop selling publications of local interest.

Glastonbury

Following the 10th century refoundation of the abbey, the development of the town probably took place in phases. There is no hint in *Domesday Book* of a market, but this does not mean that none existed. The abbey drew large numbers of pilgrims during the Saxon and medieval periods, and the need to accommodate them and the opportunity to profit from them suggest that there were facilities such as inns close to the monastery.

The monastic precinct was altered in the 12th century, making the enclosure almost as we find it today, although the Silver Street area was probably within it at that time. In 1184 a disastrous fire destroyed the *'vetusta ecclesia'*, the earliest monastic church, together with most of the abbey buildings and the valuable relics that drew the pilgrims. Perhaps as a way of funding the rebuilding work, a new town was set out during the late 12th and 13th centuries, probably reorganising the earlier settlement area. As part of this development phase, the precinct may have been altered to take the area now known as Silver Street outside the monastic enclosure.

In addition to the abbey ruins, Glastonbury retains much medieval fabric, including the monastic precinct wall, the Abbey Barn, the Tribunal, the George and Pilgrim, and St Margaret's Almshouses (formerly St Mary Magdelene, probably a leper hospital). There are many myths, legends and stories about Glastonbury that link it with King Arthur, Joseph of Arimathea, St Patrick, St Bridget and others. The links with Irish saints are the earliest documented traditions, dating from pre-Conquest times.

There are two very useful recent books - *Glastonbury* by Dr Robert Dunning and *Glastonbury* by Professor Philip Rahtz, an historian and an archaeologist respectively. Glastonbury has three excellent museums: all are well worth a visit, but the one most relevant to the medieval period is within the Abbey Visitor Centre.

33 *A conjectural reconstruction of Glastonbury Abbey circa 1500.*

Wells

King Ine founded a minster at Wells *circa* 700, on the site of a Roman mausoleum. Prehistoric evidence from the area suggests that the site already had a long history. The church was elevated to cathedral status in 909. The plantation of a new town may have followed, with a planned road system running between the cathedral and a parish church (St Cuthbert's) created to serve the town and outer parish. A medieval chapel, St Etheldreda's, stood in Southover. In the late 12th century, work began on the construction of the present cathedral. It was set on a more easterly alignment than the older Saxon church had been. The layout of the town aligns with the ancient Saxon orientation, and may pre-date the present cathedral.

By the late 12th century, Wells was a thriving town with three markets. It was the only one of Mendip's towns that was a formal medieval borough, with townsfolk holding their properties by burgage tenure. By the 14th century, it was the largest town in Somerset. An idea of the size of the population can be gained from tax records. In 1327 there were 64 tax-payers in Wells. Only those of moderate or better means paid tax, so we may be sure that in addition to the taxpayers there were many too poor to show in the records. The woollen cloth industry was of fundamental importance to the town's economy. Relations between bishop and town were at times difficult, and led in the 1340s to the walling off of the ecclesiastical area surrounding the cathedral, the Liberty. The Priory of the Hospital of St John the Baptist lay at the south-westerly end of the city.

The water that still runs through the streets of Wells was channelled into an elaborate system of water engineering works constructed for Bishop Beckington in the 15th century. It rose from St Andrew's Well close to the cathedral, and was then channelled via a stone well house and divided, 'half the water to be led towards the city, half to flow to the palace'. There were at least four mills in the town, the bishop's mill, the town mill, St John's Priory mill, and Keward mill. The great palace moat itself had a place in the water management scheme, serving as millpond and reservoir for the city mills. In later years the millers claimed the right to open and close the hatch that fed moat water into the millstream, so that in dry weather the palace had little control over the water level in the moat.

Associated with the cathedral are many important medieval buildings, including the moated Bishop's Palace, Vicars' Close, the several arched gateways, the Old Deanery, the Bishop's Barn and others. The bishop's deer park, laid out in the early 13th century, was far more extensive than the small area that is now known as the park.

Wells: A Study of Town Origins and Early Development by A.J. Scrase is a wonderfully detailed investigation of the medieval city landscape.

35 *Wells* circa *1275*.

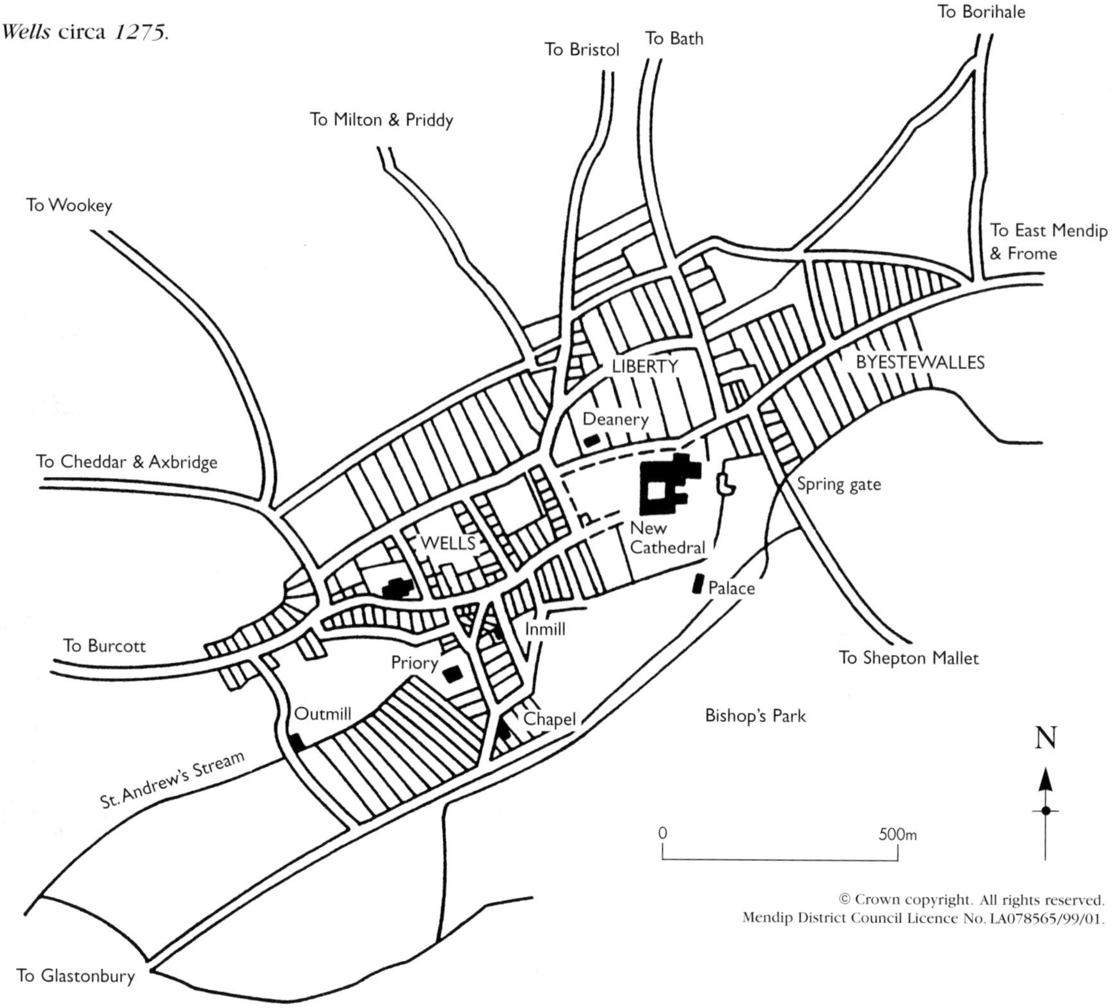

To Wookey
To Milton & Priddy
To Bristol
To Bath
To Borihale

To Cheddar & Axbridge
To East Mendip & Frome

LIBERTY
BYESTEWALLES

Deanery
Spring gate

WELLS
New Cathedral

Palace

To Burcott
Inmill
To Shepton Mallet

Priory

Outmill
Chapel
Bishop's Park

St. Andrew's Stream

N

0   500m

© Crown copyright. All rights reserved.
Mendip District Council Licence No. LA078565/99/01.

To Glastonbury

King's Castle
Tor Hill

N
W — E
S

Park Wood

Dulcote

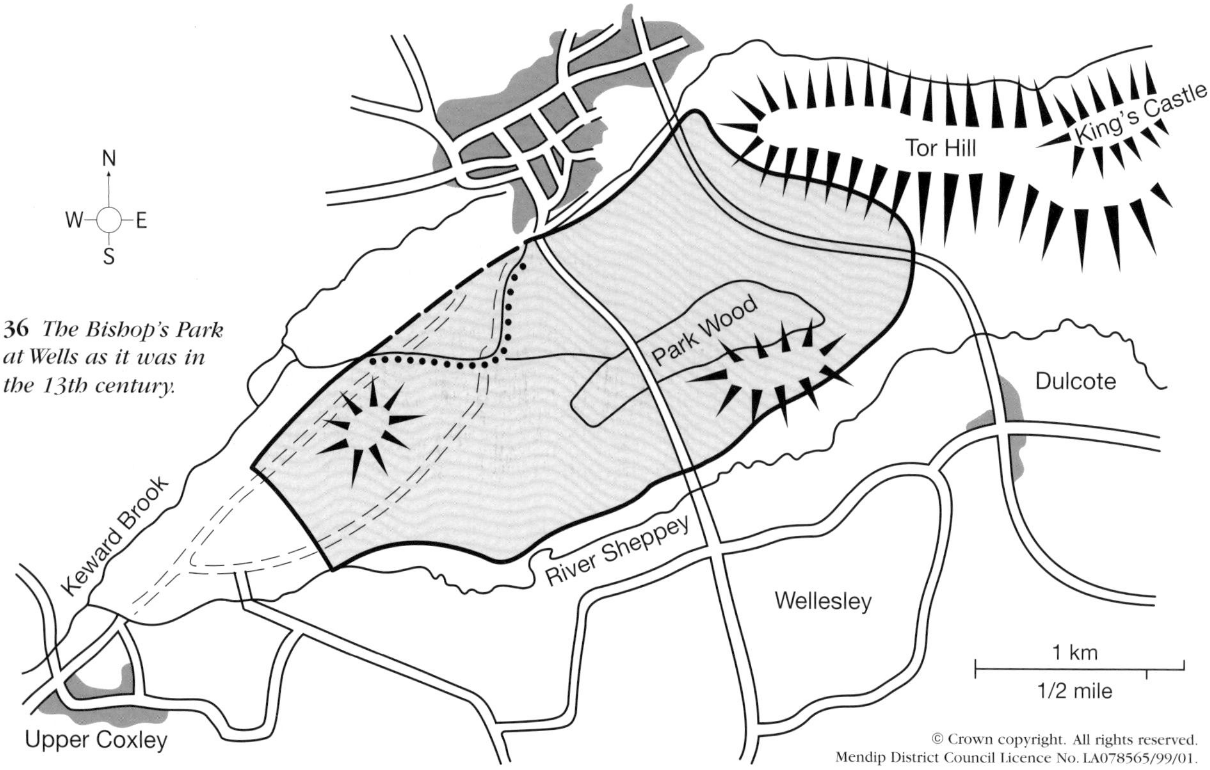

36 *The Bishop's Park at Wells as it was in the 13th century.*

Keward Brook

River Sheppey

Wellesley

1 km
1/2 mile

Upper Coxley

© Crown copyright. All rights reserved.
Mendip District Council Licence No. LA078565/99/01.

37 *The Whitstone still marks the meeting place of the medieval hundred court on Whitstone Hill.*

Shepton Mallet

There is still much that archaeological investigation can tell us about the genesis of the town at Shepton. The extent to which there may have been some continuity from the late Roman trading centre at Fosse Lane is by no means clear. The Roman site seems to have been abandoned for centuries after the post-Roman period. The parish church of St Peter and St Paul contains Saxon fabric, and the dedication itself usually indicates a pre-Conquest origin. There is no sign in *Domesday Book* of a town; rather, Shepton appears at that time to have been a subsidiary of the very large estate of Pilton.

The town may have been a speculative development by the Courcelles (later Mallets) who held the manor in the Middle Ages from Glastonbury Abbey. Interestingly, the Courcelles also held Frome, and the thriving urban centre there may have persuaded them of the profitability of setting up a new town at Shepton. A spur to Shepton's development may have been the close proximity of the hundred meeting place, the Whitstone that still stands on Whitstone Hill. The regular gatherings of men at hundred meeting places, held to carry out judicial and administrative business, would have provided a natural opportunity for marketing and exchange. Informal markets may later have been superseded by more organised events. Market and fair charters were granted for Shepton in 1235, 1260 and 1318, but these may have been confirming existing arrangements. The establishment of a regular market could have been accompanied by the setting out of regular property plots on either side of Town Street and High Street.

We know very little about Shepton in the Middle Ages because no historical research has yet been undertaken. It is the only one of Mendip's towns that has not had its medieval documents studied.

38 *Shepton's Market Cross was built circa 1500.*

CASTLES AND MOATED MANOR HOUSES

There are a number of medieval sites in Mendip that were to some extent defensive in nature. Fenny Castle, Wookey, was constructed on a small natural hill rising from low-lying land. The natural landform has been scarped, and the earthworks of a motte and bailey, with traces of a surrounding moat, survive today. A stone castle once topped the mound, but it was ruinous by the 16th century, when it was observed by John Leland. Historical references date back to the 14th century, although the motte and bailey are probably Norman of the 11th or 12th century.

Hale's Castle, Selwood, is an Anglo-Saxon or Norman ringwork with the associated earthworks of a possible bailey and field system. It is a good example of a nationally rare type of monument - fewer than 60 ringworks with baileys are known, and the survival of part of an associated field system is rare.

Nunney Castle is a moated fortified tower-house, built in the 1370s in the French style. Earthworks to the north-west of the castle may be the fragments of a bailey. The castle was attacked and taken in 1645 by Cromwell's forces, when the roof and floors were removed; but the worst damage occurred in 1910, when much of the north wall collapsed.

39 *Nunney Castle, built in the 14th century in the French style.*

Farleigh Hungerford Castle developed from a Norman manor house, fortified in the late 14th century. Originally consisting of a single court with associated buildings, an outer bailey was added a generation later. The castle includes within its walls a medieval chapel and a priest's house in addition to the main castle buildings and enclosures.

Nunney Castle and Farleigh Hungerford Castle are delightful places to visit. Both are in the care of English Heritage: you can wander freely around the ruins at Nunney, while a small admission charge is made at Farleigh.

At Marston Moat, the manor house of the Bigot family was built before 1195, but nothing now remains to be seen of the building. The moat, which is surrounded by a substantial outer bank, is a rare survival; many moats were filled in during the late medieval/post-medieval period. The moat at Spargrove survives, although it has been partly levelled, as has the moat that Skinner drew at Downhead in the 19th century. Other moated sites existed at The Priory, Ditcheat; Court Farm, Wookey; Priory Farm, West Pennard; Lottisham Manor; and possibly Pilton Manor. The best surviving moats are those at Farleigh Hungerford Castle and Nunney Castle, and the magnificent moat that surrounds the Bishop's Palace at Wells.

INDUSTRIAL LANDSCAPE FEATURES

Medieval coal-mining, quarrying and other mineral extractions have left their mark upon the Mendip landscape. Many of the pits and grooves left by lead extraction on the Mendip plateau are medieval. Bell pits - shafts with surrounding mounds of spoil - are characteristic of early coal-mining and iron extraction. The Nettlebridge valley contains some very well-preserved early coal-mining landscapes, and place name evidence suggests pre-Domesday coal-mining at the little hamlet of Pitcot near Stratton-on-the-Fosse. Glastonbury Abbey accounts show that, in the 13th century, coal was used in lime-kilns constructed for the building of a barn at Street and a sheephouse at Mells.

Some quarries date from the Middle Ages and earlier. References to stone pits on Pennard Ridge in early documents can be matched to existing quarry pits in the modern landscape; these quarries must be Saxon or Roman. The creamy oolitic limestone from St Andrew's Quarry at Doulting was used to build Wells Cathedral in the late 12th century. The quarry had been leased from Glastonbury Abbey, and when the abbey needed to be rebuilt following a disastrous fire in 1184, Doulting stone became temporarily unavailable for the cathedral. Wells was forced to change its quarry, and the change in stone source can still be traced in the different colours of the masonry on the south wall facing into the Camery. Lias stone

40 *The circular mound where a medieval windmill once stood can be seen in the centre foreground. It lies across an earlier pattern of ridge and furrow. The sharply defined lines are 18th century drainage works.*

was quarried at Street and at Evercreech, and at the latter quarry faces can be found where the fairly flat beds were exploited right up to the edges of trackways or adjacent fields, leaving a difference in level of a metre or two between quarried and unquarried land. In the east of Mendip, at Beckington and probably Norton St Philip, stone roof tiles were quarried and used from at least the 14th century.

In Mendip, surviving fords include those at Pilton, North Wootton, Chewton Mendip, Wanstrow, Easton Trow at Alhampton, Cockmill at East Pennard, and Wookey. Oldford near Frome no longer has a ford, but it was clearly an important crossing-point in the past. Fords are usually of great antiquity, marking the crossing-points of very early routes. In many cases fords were lost when the roads were bridged, but where they have survived they are places with great charm. Nettlebridge was called Nettleford in the 11th century, and beneath the 19th century bridge lies a clapper-type bridge made of three great stones; it was presumably this early bridge that occasioned the name change.

A number of medieval bridges remain, notably those at Croscombe, Tellisford, Scutts Bridge at Rode, Coleford, Murtry, Bolters Bridge at Hornblotton, and Charterhouse.

Mills have been an important part of Mendip's industrial past. Many places already had a mill by Domesday; these were grist mills, for grinding corn. From the 12th century the cloth industry made use of fulling mills, with great wooden stocks for beating the cloth until it was felted. New water mills were built to power the fulling stocks (locally, sometimes called beatles), and in some cases existing corn mills were converted for fulling. Windmills for grinding corn were built from the late 12th century; early models, post-mills, were raised up on mounds.

Walk down to the river at Tellisford to see the quaint packhorse bridge and the evocative ruins of the mill. A mill stood here by 1086, and at least 800 years of water-powered milling took place.

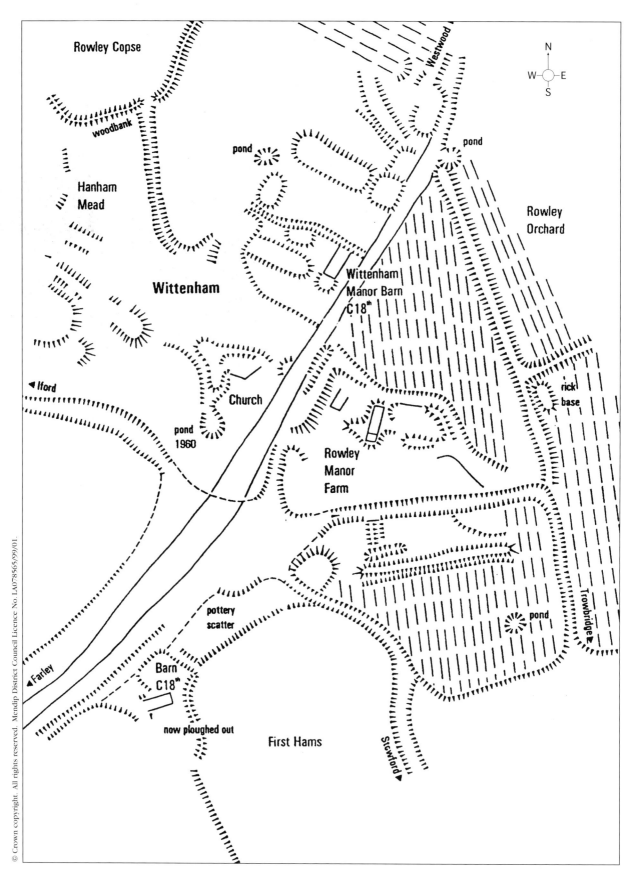

Rowley Copse

woodbank

Hanham
Mead

Wittenham

◀ Iford

Church

pond
1960

pond

Wittenham
Manor Barn
C18ᵗʰ

Rowley
Manor
Farm

Westwood

pond

Rowley
Orchard

rick
base

Trowbridge ▼

pottery
scatter

Barn
C18ᵗʰ

◀ Farley

now ploughed out

First Hams

Stowford ▼

pond

41 *The deserted medieval village of Wittenham near Farleigh Hungerford once had its own church and manor house. The settlement declined gradually, and only earthworks remain on the site today.*

A *Ashen Hill Barrows lie close to the much earlier Priddy Circles, showing that this area was the focus of special attention in the Neolithic and Bronze Age periods.*

B *Meare Fish House once stood beside a great freshwater lake. When the moors flood, the lake once again separates Meare from Godney.*

C *The moat and walls surrounding the Bishop's Palace at Wells were constructed at a time when relations between the bishop and the town were tense.*

D *The medieval squint bridge at Croscombe.*

E *The course of the River Brue was altered in the early Middle Ages, but its old meandering course can still be seen when the ground becomes waterlogged.*

F *The hedgerow in the centre of the photograph is the western boundary of Glastonbury Abbey's medieval deer park at Pilton, established in the late 12th or early 13th century.*

G *One of several early maps of Mendip. This version was redrawn from a 17th century map which was part of Ashwick court rolls.*

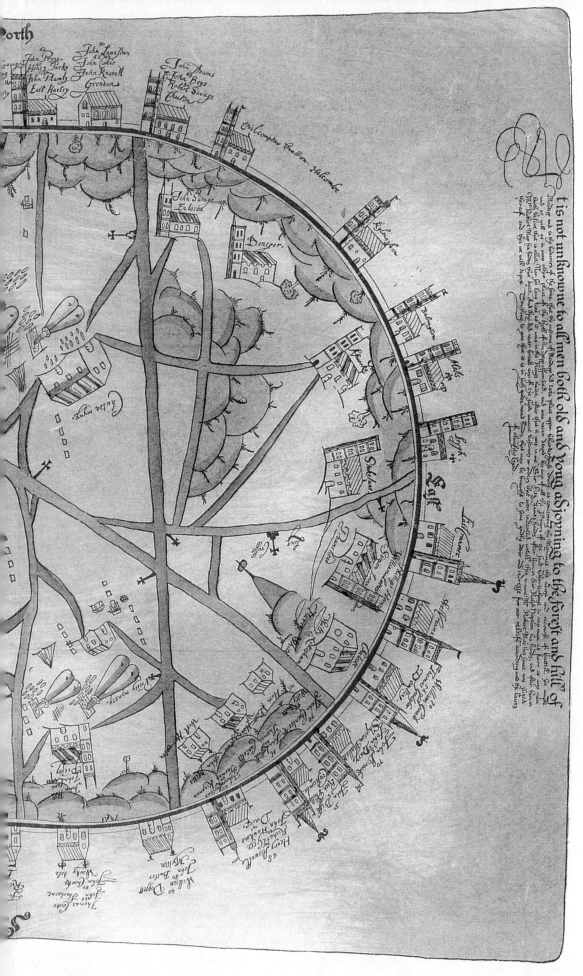

H *The Roman road from the Fosse Way to the temple at Lamyatt can still be seen terraced into the hillside along the parish boundary between East Pennard and Ditcheat. It was described in the 10th century as the 'miclan dic', the large dyke.*

I *Fairlady Well, Priddy, a spring used as a medieval parish boudary marker.*

J *Newbury colliery winding-house.*

K *Fussell's Ironworks, Mells, an important industrial heritage site.*

L *Lead-mining on Mendip has created beautiful and fascinating landscape features.*

M *The moat and curtain wall of Farleigh Hungerford Castle.*

N *Effigies in Farleigh Hungerford Castle Chapel.*

CHAPTER 8

YESTERDAY'S MENDIP

POST-MEDIEVAL

1540 onwards

The cultural change at the end of the Middle Ages, of which the dissolution of the monasteries was but a part, heralded many and far-reaching changes in the everyday life of Mendip folk. Many of these were manifested in the landscape, testifying to a period of tremendous technological advance and social and economic metamorphosis.

At a national level, the balance between rural and urban populations altered dramatically. The great mass of the medieval population were country dwellers, but by the turn of the 20th century most people lived in towns. In Mendip the move from country to town did take place, but to a lesser degree, perhaps because of the more limited opportunities offered by the small towns here and the industrial nature of some the larger villages, such as Croscombe and Beckington.

Industries had always been important locally, but the Industrial Revolution brought challenges to established patterns of working, and caused unrest and hardship for many. The decline of the local textile industry during the 19th century is attributed mainly to a failure to embrace technological advance, leaving the West Country unable to compete with the vigorous northern production centres. Eventually mechanisation did take place locally, and factory production increasingly replaced cottage industry, leaving a heritage of larger industrial premises, virtually all of which were later absorbed into other industrial processes.

Linked to the Industrial Revolution was the development of transport and communications systems alongside the organisation of public utilities and services including water and sewage provision, power supplies, health and educational facilities.

In the countryside the two movements that gave rise to the most profound changes were gentry-led; the improvement of agriculture accompanied by the taming and enclosure of the wetland and upland pastures, and the creation of idealised and beautified landscapes.

Building traditions, both rural and urban, saw a revolution during the period. The movement described by the pioneering landscape historian W. G. Hoskins as the 'Great Rebuilding' saw the abandonment of medieval domestic arrangements. Open-hall houses gave way to buildings with upper storeys. The division of dwellings into a number of rooms gave much greater privacy and comfort. Timber-framed building techniques were replaced first by stone and later also by brick, although - in contrast to some parts of England - stone buildings were relatively common here by the later Middle Ages.

ECCLESIASTICAL SITES AND BUILDINGS

Ecclesiastical changes in the post-medieval period encompassed the re-use and demolition of monastic buildings and chantry chapels, the construction of new urban churches, the growth of Nonconformity with its numerous chapels, and the re-introduction of Roman Catholic churches.

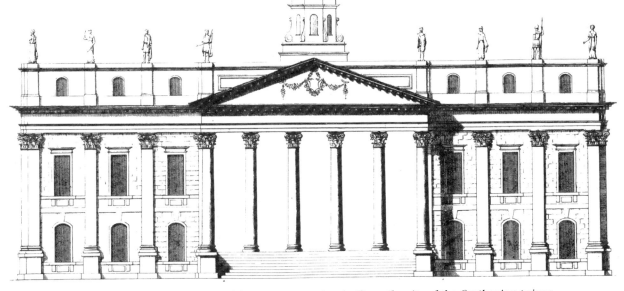

42 *Witham House, the early 18th century mansion built on the site of the Carthusian priory.*

The dissolution of the monasteries in the 16th century was accompanied by the wholesale destruction of many ecclesiastical buildings. Mendip's monasteries at Glastonbury and Witham Friary both had a phase of partial re-occupation, and both were subsequently used as convenient stone quarries.

At Witham, no standing structures remain on the main priory site. Part of the monastic church was incorporated into a later mansion, but the mansion itself no longer stands. There are valuable archaeological remains below ground, while on the surface are the humps and bumps of earthworks. The precinct that enclosed the monastery is still recognisable, although a railway line bisects the field. The monastic fishponds remain in good condition, while in the village the lay brothers' church and a dovecote still stand. After the dissolution of the priory it was converted into a residence by one of Thomas Cromwell's advisers, Ralph Hopton. By the early 18th century, part of the monastery had probably been incorporated in an elegant mansion built for the Wyndham family, but most of the medieval buildings seem to have been demolished. During the 1860s the Wyndham mansion itself fell into disrepair, and the new estate owner, William Beckford, Lord Mayor of London, began constructing a yet grander mansion in an adjacent field, to a design by Robert Adam. It was abandoned before completion, and only humps and bumps in the grass remain today to tell of the site's 600-year history of fine buildings.

Glastonbury Abbey was the last Somerset monastery to be dissolved. Afterwards, the buildings housed a religious community of over 40 families of Flemish clothmakers for a brief stay of about two years. Resources and building improvements which had been promised to them by the Duke of Somerset were not forthcoming, and the group failed to flourish. After a brief and somewhat unhappy residence, they left the abbey site and eventually moved to Frankfurt. The monastic ruins were extensively quarried for stone, and medieval masonry from the abbey can be seen in many local buildings. Much of the rubble was used for road stone; the raised causeway across low-lying land between Glastonbury and Wells is said to have been built of monastic stone. Despite this damage, substantial ruins, the precinct enclosure, the earthworks and the archaeology below ground make Glastonbury

43 Glastonbury Abbey was dissolved in 1539.

Abbey an archaeological site of prime importance. In the early 20th century it was bought by the Church of England, and since 1908 it has been in the care of trustees whose aim is to conserve the site and ruins.

The expansion of urban populations in the post-medieval period left medieval churches unable to accommodate the increased congregations of the 18th and 19th centuries. The construction of new Church of England churches in towns reflects this increased demand - Christchurch, Frome, is a good example. At Rode a new church was built in the 19th century because the settlement straddled the county boundary between Wiltshire and Somerset, and there was no convenient church on the Wiltshire side. Christchurch, Rode, no longer lies in Wiltshire, as the boundary has since been altered.

44 Christchurch, Rode, was built in 1824 close to the county boundary so that Wiltshire people need not attend church in Somerset.

The growth of Nonconformity from the 17th century was an important force socially as well as spiritually, as most social life was centred on church or chapel. In the early days, Nonconformist religious meetings often took place out of doors or in private houses. In Croscombe, Nonconformist meetings were first held at the roadside, high above the river valley settlement; a small enclosed burial ground can still be found close to the meeting place. As the movement grew stronger, Nonconformist chapels were built throughout Mendip, and often several chapels were to be found even in small parishes.

In the countryside the gentry and squirarchy tended to remain staunchly Church of England. In towns and in strongly industrialised villages, Nonconformity was supported by a broader cross-section of society. The grand architecture of many urban chapels reflects the wealth and refined tastes of their congregations.

45 *Rook Lane Chapel, Frome, dating from 1707, was built in such a grand style that it was a source of controversy among Frome townspeople, and at times of trouble a mob would gather and cry 'Down with the cupola'.*

Quakers, otherwise known as the Society of Friends, have been an influential part of the Street community for three centuries. In 1655 'several ... faythfull servants and ministers from the Counteys of Westmorland and Lancaster' travelled to Somerset to preach the gospel. Members of the local farming community were drawn to the new faith, and by 1656 a regular Street meeting had been formed, with monthly meetings at East Lydford. The graceful Quaker Meeting House in Street was built in 1860 on an established site.

Roman Catholic churches were absent from England from the Reformation until the 18th century. Downside Abbey is Mendip's most famous Roman Catholic church, a fascinating and beautiful building. The house and estate were bought in 1814 by a community from Douai, which fled to England in 1795 because of the dangers presented to the monks and boys by the French Revolution. They moved first to Acton Burnell, Shropshire, then to Downside. Buildings were added as the school and community expanded. The main church was started in 1872, the chancel was built between 1901 and 1905, and the nave, designed by Sir Giles Gilbert Scott, was begun in 1923.

THE POST-MEDIEVAL TOWNS OF MENDIP
The wealth of Mendip's towns throughout the later Middle Ages, and for most of the post-medieval period, was based on the thriving cloth industry of east Somerset and west Wiltshire. Wool produced on the Mendip Hills and elsewhere was spun, dyed and woven by craftsmen working either for themselves or as out-workers for wealthy clothiers. Cloth was processed in the many fulling mills that were situated along the rivers and fast-flowing streams.

Markets and fairs for the sale of wool, cloth and dyestuffs, as well as foodstuffs, livestock and manufactured goods, were held not only in the towns but also in a number of semi-urban villages such as Croscombe, Nunney, Beckington, and Norton St Philip. The increasing availability of manufactured goods during the period led to the expansion of trade and commerce; permanent shops provided goods and services previously offered only periodically at markets and fairs.

Urban Housing
Town populations grew, and with this expansion came new housing development. Between 1660 and 1695 the number of rateable inhabitants of Frome increased by at least four times.

'The town of Froom ... is so prodigiously increased within these last twenty or thirty year, that they have built a new church, and so many new streets of houses, and those houses are so full of inhabitants, that Frome is now reckoned to have more people in it than the city of Bath, and some say, than even Salisbury itself, and if their trade continues to increase for a few years more, as it has done for those past, it is likely to be one of the greatest and wealthiest inland towns in England.' **Daniel Defoe, 1720s.**

The area now called Trinity is an early development of industrial housing. It was investigated and surveyed in 1976 by the Royal Commission on Historical Monuments together with local researchers. The development of a greenfield site took place over a period of some 60 years from 1665. Analysis of the plots and buildings shows that the development was originally fairly high-status, but that the property plots grew smaller and the buildings more modest as time went on. The buildings themselves contain little physical evidence of their use. Presumably they were dual-purpose buildings, serving as domestic accommodation as well as workshops, but the way in which the interior space was used is not clear. Few of the surviving buildings had large windows to cast light onto looms, and none had mansard roofs to allow more storage and work space in the loft. It seems most likely that clothworking was carried out in unheated ground-floor rooms adjacent to the main living-room.

An inventory of the Vallis Way home of John Jelly, clothier, made in 1724, gives a vivid picture of the interior arrangements of local houses at the time. On the ground floor was 'a kitchen, little inner room, hall, pantry, cellar, brewhouse'; on the first floor, 'a best chamber, kitchen chamber and a little chamber'; and above were the 'garrotts and wool loft'. The 'sheare shop' was presumably a separate building within the curtilage.

46 *Trinity Street, Frome, was built between 1718 and 1722, part of an early industrial housing development. The church is later.*

The Trinity and Sheppard's Barton areas of Frome are well worth a visit. The narrow streets and terraced houses are little altered from the 17th and 18th centuries, when they housed many families dependent on the textile industry. Before you visit, look at the splendid book *Early Industrial Housing: The Trinity Area of Frome,* published by the Royal Commission on Historical Monuments.

Trinity was a speculative development, not tied to any particular employer. A contrast is found in the industrial housing built by the wealthy Sheppard family, clothiers of Frome, who provided artisans' accommodation at Sheppard's Barton for their own workers. In Shepton Mallet, Garston Street and Town

Lane are developments of weavers' cottages built in the 17th century.

Industrial housing provision in Street covers a range of types. During the 19th century, Street developed from a quiet rural village into a thriving shoe-making centre. In 1825 it had a small farming and quarrying population, but by the turn of the 20th century 1,200 workers lived and worked there. Cottages built for shoe outworkers by Cyrus Clark in 1860 had workshops for shoe-making at first-floor level above their back sculleries. Many terraces of houses were built for Clarks workers over the years, most of them to a high quality of design and construction. From 1911 onwards, council housing was built by the Street Urban District Council; it was among the earliest in the country, and attractive in style and setting.

47 *Housing in the Arts and Crafts style provided in Street for Clarks workers in 1889.*

At the upper end of the scale of urban housing are the gracious buildings that were once the homes of wealthy clothiers, mill owners, merchants, clergy and other gentry. Wells, Shepton Mallet and Frome each have a wonderful heritage of fine domestic buildings. Very often these houses stood close beside their owners' industrial premises and workers' accommodation. The grand clothier's home of Sales House, Shepton Mallet, is part of a group of buildings that once comprised mill, dye-house, shops and cottages. The elegant town houses at Willow Vale, Frome, are flanked by workshops and more humble workers' accommodation.

48 *18th century Sales House, Shepton Mallet, a clothier's home that once stood close beside the mill, dye-house, workshops and workers' cottages of its proprietor. This proximity of industry to both high- and low-status domestic accommodation was typical of many such units in both town and country.*

Public Buildings

The prosperity of Mendip's towns in the 17th, 18th and 19th centuries is reflected in the architectural legacy of these periods. Public buildings such as the town halls of Glastonbury and Wells, and semi-public buildings such as the Market House and the Blue House in Frome, are important features of our town centres. The building of the Pump House in 1754 marked the beginning of Glastonbury's history as a minor spa, and interest in the curative properties of Glastonbury's springs continues to this day. A building with less pleasant associations is the prison at Shepton Mallet, built as the county gaol in 1610.

49 *Glastonbury's 18th century spa Pump House.*

50 *The Blue House, Frome, an almshouse and school built in 1728.*

Urban Industries

Industries that were important in Mendip towns included beer and cider brewing, card-making (the cards were used in cloth production), cloth, crêpe and silk production, the hand-knitting of stockings, tanning and leather-working, shoe-making, metal-working (Cockey's and Singer's at Frome), printing (Butler and Tanner, Frome), and brick-making (Glastonbury). The buildings and sites connected with all of these industries are a valuable element of the local historic landscape.

Industrial buildings such as factories and warehouses document the area's economic history, and are often interesting and attractive architecturally. The former Anglo-Bavarian Brewery in Shepton Mallet is a fascinating building which makes a strong contribution to the town. The unusual central buildings of Clarks shoe-making factory at Street owe their inspiration to the Arts and Crafts movement of the late 19th century. There are many other important urban industrial buildings in Mendip, including the old Butler and Tanner Works at Trinity, the Lamb Brewery and Merchants Barton Silk Mill in Frome, the former Showerings factory and the several mills in Shepton Mallet.

***The Anglo* by Fred Davis is a fascinating account of the history of the unusual brewery buildings that stand so close to the heart of Shepton Mallet.**

51 *A metalwork dragon made by Singer's of Frome.*

Early Town Planning

From the late 18th century, various urban public works were carried out. In Frome a brave and early example of town planning was introduced, inspired by Thomas Bunn, a local man of vision with an enthusiastic commitment to the development of the town. His ambitious plan included two major undertakings, the construction of North Parade in 1797, and of Bath Street in the early 19th century. Bath Street cut through the earlier street pattern, taking a gentler gradient up the otherwise steep slope from the river crossing. It was carefully landscaped, with boundary walls decorated with elaborate piers. A new screen and west front was added to St John's Church at this time, part of the general townscape enhancement. Several cedar trees were planted as part of this work, the sole survivor having been planted in 1814.

52 *Crispin Hall was built in 1885 to provide a public hall, library and reading-room for the people of Street.*

In both Wells and Glastonbury, old buildings were demolished close to the present Town Halls. With their removal to create more spacious street areas, both towns lost medieval buildings that would certainly be valued elements of the modern townscape had they survived. In Street, Leigh Road was developed as an area devoted to public buildings. Crispin Hall (which incorporated a public hall, library, reading-room, museum and gymnasium), the public library, the vestry rooms, the technical school, and the later Maxime Cinema cluster together in a little group, forming a focus for the settlement centre.

Services, Utilities and Institutions

The development of community services and public utilities dates from the 19th century onwards. Early arrangements for gas and electricity supply, sewers and clean water, fire brigades, schools, hospitals and workhouses, all have left their mark in the historic fabric of Mendip's towns. Some have been replaced or superseded, whilst others continue to be used for their original purpose.

Public Parks

The provision of parks and gardens for public recreation took place from the late 19th century. All of Mendip's towns have a number of parks and play areas, each with a unique character and history. The Recreation Ground in Wells was created in celebration of Queen Victoria's Jubilee in 1887. It was funded by public subscription, with both the mayor and the bishop making especially large contributions. Bishop Hervey had a romantic and enthusiastic view of the venture: 'Summer evenings passed in the beautiful open air, with the amusement of looking on at the cricket, and perhaps with a band of music occasionally, would promote an innocent cheerfulness of spirit which is almost a step towards godliness'.

In Shepton Mallet Sir Ernest Jardine provided a large and delightful garden for the families of workers in his factory in the early years of the 20th century. The old millpond was converted into an ornamental lake, and a boat was provided. A little colony of fancy waterfowl was established The garden has since then twice fallen into disrepair and subsequently been renovated. Jardine's park was a private amenity, but the general population of Shepton was, as it still is, well served by the Collett Park, open to all.

THE RURAL LANDSCAPE
Settlement

Many changes in rural settlement occurred in the post-medieval period. The development of new industrial areas brought with it the need for new housing. In some places this consisted of only a few cottages, but elsewhere there was substantial settlement growth. Coleford, now quite a large village, was once a small hamlet, which expanded with the growth of the local coal-mining industry. At Wookey Hole the present settlement was created to accommodate workers at the paper mill and largely dates from the 19th century, although a small settlement already existed there.

Busy industrial hamlets grew up at Bowlish and Darshill close to Shepton. At Bowlish a fine clothier's house stood close beside its two mills, storage buildings, workers' cottages and former millpond. Further down the valley at Darshill, the millpond and the workers' cottages can still be found, together with other industrial relics, including an earlier millpond or holding pond. Some industrial dwellings were short-lived, abandoned with the closure of their workplaces. At Stoke Bottom the abandoned hamlet of Fernhill stands close to a deserted paper mill, disused quarry, coal mines and ruinous mansion house.

53 *This ornamental garden in Shepton was created for his factory workers by Sir Ernest Jardine.*

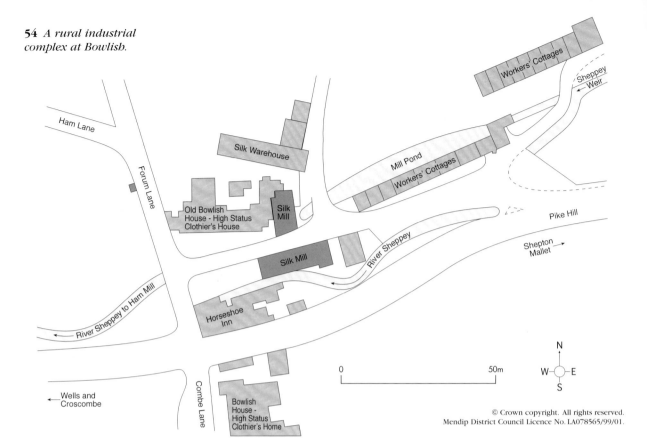

54 *A rural industrial complex at Bowlish.*

In the image:
Ham Lane
Forum Lane
Silk Warehouse
Workers' Cottages
Sheppey Weir
Mill Pond
Workers' Cottages
Old Bowlish House - High Status Clothier's House
Silk Mill
Pike Hill
River Sheppey
Shepton Mallet
Silk Mill
River Sheppey to Ham Mill
Horseshoe Inn
Wells and Croscombe
Combe Lane
Bowlish House - High Status Clothier's Home
0   50m
N W E S

Following the enclosure and improvement of the Mendip plateau and low-lying moors, new farmsteads were built in these areas, altering the established settlement pattern of a ring of nucleated settlements surrounding the wetlands and uplands.

Settlements were dynamic - expanding and contracting in response to changes in population density and local economic opportunities. In some places the focus of settlement shifted, as at Holcombe, where the present village developed well away from the medieval site, leaving the Norman parish church standing alone among the earthworks of the deserted dwellings.

Some medieval farmsteads and hamlets were abandoned; in many cases this was due to changes in agricultural arrangements, particularly the amalgamation of small landholdings into larger farm units. Occasionally, small settlements were replanned and rebuilt to create picturesque estate villages - almost all the cottages in the villages of Doulting and Downhead were rebuilt in the 19th century, by the Paget and the Portman estates respectively.

Long, narrow roadside plots and encroachments on open spaces are characteristic of land appropriated by squatters in the post-medieval period. Squatter plots generally represent the dwellings of a section of society that lay outside the landholding rural community - labourers, servants, and craftsmen.

During the Middle Ages, houses of higher status - usually manor houses - were almost invariably sited next to the parish church or manorial chapel, with a village or hamlet close at hand. From the 18th century, it became fashionable to create fine country houses away from settlement centres. At Mells a mansion was newly built in an extensive park, while the ancient manor house beside the church was rented out to a farmer. In some places existing settlements were re-moved to make way for parks and provide the desired isolated setting. This happened at Babbington, Orchardleigh and Marston. Mendip has a splendid heritage of country mansions, including Ammerdown near Kilmersdon, Southill at Cranmore, and Ston Easton. The high cost of maintaining such properties has meant that several have been fully or partly demolished - Ashwick Grove at Oakhill, Stoke House at Stoke Bottom, and Charlton House near Kilmersdon among them. The efforts of the various conservation bodies and local authorities ensure that the loss of such important buildings would not occur today.

Orchardleigh is a good place to visit, as you can enjoy the extensive parkland and views of the elegant mansion from the network of foot-paths that run through the estate.

55 *The ruins of Georgian Ashwick Grove, once the home of John Billingsley, an influential agricultural improver and industrialist.*

Farming

The post-medieval period saw great changes in land tenure. In the Middle Ages, land was held by lords, some great and powerful, others of only local importance. Small farmers and cottagers held their own modest portions of land through agreement with their lords, either as customary or leasehold tenures. Large estates were progressively broken up through the post-medieval period. From the mid-19th century, but particularly after the First World War, the process accelerated rapidly, so that today the land in most parishes is owned by a multiplicity of farmers, smallholders and householders.

56 *Lord Hugh Fortescue, lord of Croscombe and Ashwick, was one of the earliest landowners to enclose the Mendip uplands by Act of Parliament.*

Field systems also altered greatly. The process of enclosure of arable land, in progress from at least the 13th century, gathered speed. Well before the main enclosure thrust of the late 18th century, most of the arable land of the area had been enclosed by agreement. The 50 years from 1770 saw Acts of Parliament enabling enclosure of most of the remaining common land. Parliamentary enclosure landscapes are recognisable from their characteristically geometrical field pattern, which resulted from the apportionment of land by mapping the area and dividing it into regular shares. The patterns of rectilinear fields enclosed by straight drystone walls, thorn hedges, or rhynes, were formed in the late 18th and early 19th centuries. The geometrical woodland areas of the Mendip plateau are also of this date, planted for game cover, to act as windbreaks, and to provide cash crops.

Enclosure and improvement farming transformed the character of both the upland pastures and the low-lying wetlands. Agricultural improvement techniques were employed to bring these areas into arable cultivation. Small quarries and lime-kilns were numerous on the plateau and escarpment, as the improvement of the Mendip soils required copious applications of lime. Ponds, field barns and stock shelters are among the countryside features created as part of the enclosure movement.

Some impressive lime-kilns can be found in Vallis Vale near Frome. These particularly fine examples have been designated as listed buildings, but most lime-kilns are unprotected.

The mechanisation of farming had a major impact on the countryside. Perhaps most immediately noticeable was a dramatic reduction in labour needs: the introduction of equipment such as threshing machines, tractors, hedgetrimmers and milking machines meant that far fewer workers were needed on the land than ever before. Restricted agricultural opportunities caused many to leave the countryside and seek employment in towns, a movement that is documented in the falling population figures for rural parishes in the census returns of the 19th century. Many of the country cottages that have disappeared since the tithe maps were compiled were lost because of the plummeting employment potential of rural areas.

Machinery made it relatively easy to remove unwanted countryside features, to level uneven ground, take out hedgerows to create larger fields, and fill in millstreams and ponds. This tidying up of farmland has destroyed, often unwittingly, many valuable archaeological sites and features. The casual loss of ancient features in the countryside has been enormous over the last 50 years.

57 *In Beacon Wood visitors can find the ring-shaped earthwork that once surrounded a circular woodland.*

Gentrification of the Countryside

The creation of aesthetically pleasing countryside features and landscape areas was widespread during the 18th and 19th centuries. The creation of parks and gardens was a part of this movement, but equally important were the plantation of indigenous and exotic trees, and the building of follies, bridges, picturesque turnpike cottages and other features.

Two examples of attractively landscaped woodland plantations are to be found at Beacon Wood above Shepton Mallet, and at the Round Clump above Wells. Both these plantations are circular, the shape being defined by a drystone wall at the Round Clump and an earthen bank at Beacon Wood, and were clearly designed as distinctive landscape features. Both were planted in the late 18th or early 19th century by wealthy landowning members of the Wells gentry. Each was a dual purpose enterprise, delivering a cash crop in the long term while adding a patrician character to the landscape. Many more examples could be cited of ornamental plantings, from the sweet chestnuts that lined the northern perimeter of Downhead Park to the beeches on the boundaries of Cranmore Wood.

The post-medieval period saw great interest in the creation of grand gardens with vistas and architectural features. Seventeenth century gardens were formal,

with terraces, raised walks, knot gardens, and - where possible - viewing mounds and gazebos providing prospects of the wider countryside. The grandest gardens of this period looked out upon an extensive park, formally planted with trees, with geometrically designed paths or rides between planted blocks of fruit trees. In the 18th century, garden fashions changed, and naturalistic landscaped parks replaced formal plantings. A return to more formal arrangements with planted flower beds occurred in the 19th century. Among Mendip's best-known ornamental structures in the wider countryside is the Cranmore Tower, built by Sir John Paget in the 19th century in pursuit of his scientific interest in astronomy, but which also provided picturesque accommodation for banqueting or picnicking parties sallying forth from the Pagets' home at East Cranmore.

The earthen terraces and mounds of 17th century gardens set within a park survived at Hardington until the 1980s, but have now been destroyed. At Ashwick Grove the ruined mansion stands abandoned among the terraces and paths, the overgrown yew avenue and tangled exotic shrubs that once formed a manicured formal garden. Mendip has a number of very fine parks and gardens, nine of which feature on English Heritage's *Register of Parks and Gardens of Special Historic Interest*. Ammerdown is the grandest of the parks to have survived without damage. Orchardleigh and Ston Easton, both important historic parks, have each undergone landscape changes to accommodate golf courses during recent years.

Woodlands and Orchards

The post-medieval period saw the loss of some old woodlands and the establishment of some new ones in Mendip. The net result has probably been a slight rise in woodland cover during this period. The central plateau area of Mendip, as mentioned earlier, has probably not been heavily wooded since the Bronze Age. Eastern Mendip, especially the Selwood ridge, was quite well wooded after that period, but medieval clearances removed great swathes of tree-cover from the wide strip of lower land adjacent to the ridge.

A large wood is depicted on 17th century maps at Southwood near Baltonsborough, and medieval documents tell us that many of the villeins on Glastonbury Abbey's estate had a duty to cart wood from Baltonsborough to the monastery. The small woodlands of Park Wood and Westwood Grove are all that now remain. The deer parks of Norwood, Pilton, Evercreech and Sharpham all lost their woodlands when they were converted to farmland. Mendip's largest ancient woodland, Asham, is now perhaps a third of its early medieval size.

In the late 18th and early 19th centuries there were a number of new plantations, mainly on recently enclosed land, such as Beacon Wood and Cranmore Wood. Following the setting up of the Forestry Commission after the Second World War, new plantations were established on the Mendip plateau: Rowberrow, Stockhill and East Harptree. In some places ancient deciduous woodlands have been partly or wholly replaced with conifers, as at Harridge Wood West near Ashwick, and Ham Wood near Croscombe.

Orchards were a notable landscape feature of some parts of the district in the 18th and 19th centuries. There had been small orchards in medieval gardens, but the large areas of orchard shown on the maps of the 19th century were a recent and short-lived phenomenon, probably the result of paying agricultural wages partly in cider. Many orchards have been lost over the past 50 years, making the survivors all the more precious.

58 *The landscaped park at Orchardleigh.*

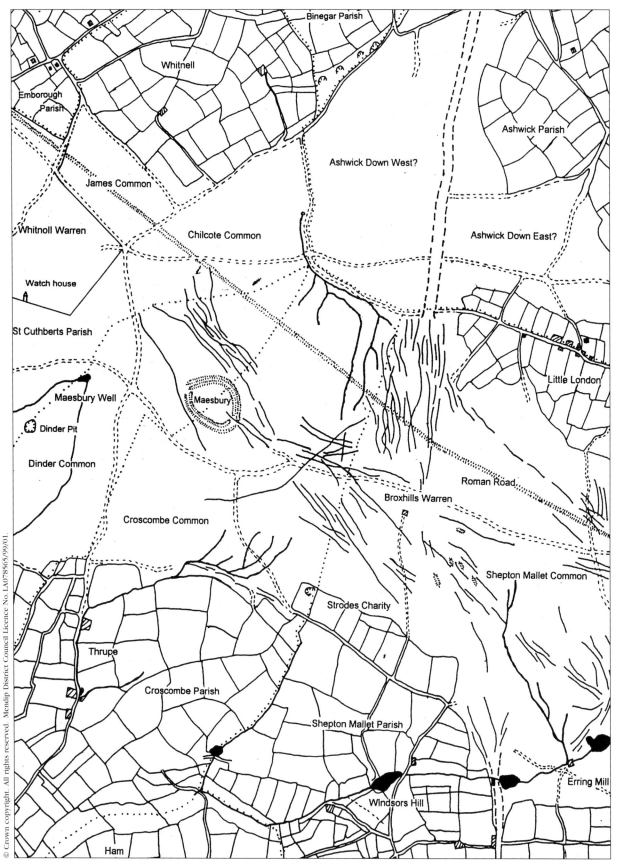

Binegar Parish

Whitnell

Emborough Parish

Ashwick Parish

Ashwick Down West?

James Common

Whitnoll Warren

Chilcote Common

Ashwick Down East?

Watch house

St Cuthberts Parish

Little London

Maesbury Well

Maesbury

Dinder Pit

Dinder Common

Roman Road

Broxhills Warren

Croscombe Common

Shepton Mallet Common

Strodes Charity

Thrupe

Croscombe Parish

Shepton Mallet Parish

Erring Mill

Windsors Hill

Ham

59 *The area north of Shepton Mallet was enclosed in the 18th century. It is deeply rutted with ancient droving tracks and roads known as holloways.*

Industrial Sites and Landscapes

The landscape of Mendip is rich in post-medieval industrial remains, particularly of lead-working, quarrying, coal-mining, peat extraction, paper-making, leather-working, brewing, metal-working, and the industries producing ceramics, textiles and edge-tools. Changes in communications and transport have left a legacy of turnpike toll houses, roads and tracks, abandoned stretches of a partly built canal, disused railways, trolleyways and inclined planes.

An excellent study, which is highly recommended, is *Somerset Roads: The Legacy of the Turnpikes* by J.B. Bentley and B.J. Murless.

Communications and Transport

Developments in transport were closely linked to the Industrial Revolution. The expansion of large, mechanised manufacturing industries, the growing importance of regional manufacturing specialisms and the increased volume of commerce and trade were made possible by improvements in the transport infrastructure.

Roads and tracks had developed over time to meet the needs of long-distance travel, local inter-settlement contact and trade, and access to landscape resources such as fields, woodlands and pastures. Across the open, upland area of Mendip, routes were not built roads (except for the Roman roads), but were ill-defined trackways, often involving a number of tracks running in parallel. Where the ground became worn by traffic, the tracks became deeply cut into the land surface, forming holloways. These holloways can be identified on aerial photographs. They are especially easy to see close to areas where enclosed land bordered open downland.

The turnpike trusts were formed in the 18th century to improve the road network. Previously, parishes had been responsible for the upkeep of roads, a duty that was not popular and often neglected. In 1624 the 'great beaten way in the parish of Wookey' had grown 'so fownderous that neither strangers nor borderers cann passe on horse or foote to Church, markett or els where ... without endangering them selves or theire cattle'.

The trusts resurfaced existing roads, re-routed them where necessary, and built new sections. Apart from the roads themselves, the trusts have left a legacy of mileposts, turnpike cottages and territorial markers. A number of trusts operated in the Mendip area, including the Black Dog, Bruton, Frome, Radstock, Shepton Mallet, Trowbridge, Wells and Westbury Trusts. The pioneering road builder John Loudon McAdam was the surveyor retained by the Shepton Mallet Trust.

The trustees were disappointed by his performance as he appeared only three times in three years, and the end of his contract was greeted with some relief.

There were many changes to the network of roads and lanes in the post-medieval period, not all linked to turnpiking activity. Some trackways leading to communal meadows or open fields became obsolete when the land was enclosed, and went out of use. Other roads were created as part of Parliamentary enclosure activity. Footpaths were established by workers making their way to quarries, collieries, lead-works and other industrial sites.

During the 18th century's national bout of 'Canal Fever', the Dorset and Somerset Canal was planned. It was to form a link between the River Avon and Poole Harbour by joining the Kennet and Avon Canal with the River Stour near Sturminster Newton, with a branch reaching westwards to serve the collieries of the Nettlebridge valley by bringing their coal to Frome. The project foundered and the main canal was never built, but most of the Nettlebridge-Frome stretch was constructed. The bed of the canal, with various bridges, basins, retaining walls and aqueducts, can still be found. The two best-known structures of the canal are the Huckeyduck at Coleford and Murtry Aqueduct near Frome. Murtry is an especially fine structure, built of creamy freestone in a genteel 18th century style.

60 *The line of the Dorset and Somerset Canal at Vobster Cross.*

Dorſet and Somerſet Canal.

No. 312.

Purſuant to an Act of Parliament paſſed in the Thirty-ſixth Year of the Reign of King GEORGE the IIId. intituled,

" An Act for making a Navigable Canal from or near Gains-Crofs, in the Pariſh of Shillingſton-
" Okeford, in the County of Dorſet, to communicate with the Kennet and Avon Canal, at
" or near Widbrook, in the County of Wilts, and alfo a certain Navigable Branch from the
" intended Canal."

This Ticket Certifies that *James Martin of Stalbridge in the County of Dorset Gentleman* is a Subſcriber to this Undertaking, and entitled to a Share therein, numbered *312*.

In Teſtimony whereof the Common Seal of the Company is hereunto affixed this *twenty first* Day of *June* One Thouſand Seven Hundred and Ninety *six*

} CLERKS TO THE
SAID COMPANY.

61 *A Dorset and Somerset Canal share certificate issued in 1796.*

Try **The Dorset and Somerset Canal: An Illustrated History** by Ken Clew for an excellent read. Most of the bed of the abandoned canal - together with various bridges and aqueducts - can be found, although in some places it has been damaged or destroyed. Coleford and Murtry are good places to explore the remains.

From the 1850s a railway network of some complexity developed in the Mendip area, eventually becoming simplified to operate as the Great Western and the Somerset and Dorset Joint, with a number of small mineral lines serving collieries, quarries and the Oakhill Brewery. The railways brought social and economic change in Mendip, as elsewhere, by opening distant markets to agricultural and industrial producers alike. The vastly increased speed and affordability of personal travel encouraged the development of tourism, and made working away from home an easier option. The railways also had a strong impact on the urban landscape, cutting through long-established street and property patterns, and encouraging the establishment of industrial premises close to stations.

Wells had three railway stations, and although they have long since ceased operation, their influence on the development of adjacent areas of the city is still in evidence.

Dr Beeching's 1960s retrenchment plan hastened the already existent decline of the railway system. The Somerset and Dorset suffered a slow demise as investment and maintenance were withheld and services cut. There was considerable local opposition to the closure of the railway, but, in spite of this, all services had ceased by 1973.

Lead-Working

Mendip has some unique and exciting lead-working landscapes which have developed over at least 2,000 years. Lead-mining reached its post-Roman peak in the 17th century, and by the early 19th century lead was no longer mined in any quantity on Mendip. During the 19th century Cornish engineers came to Mendip hoping to rejuvenate the industry. No substantial quantities of ore were recovered, and it seems that by that time Mendip's lead had been almost completely worked out.

62 *St Cuthbert's Lead Works, Priddy, the last of the Victorian re-smelting enterprises, closed in 1908.*

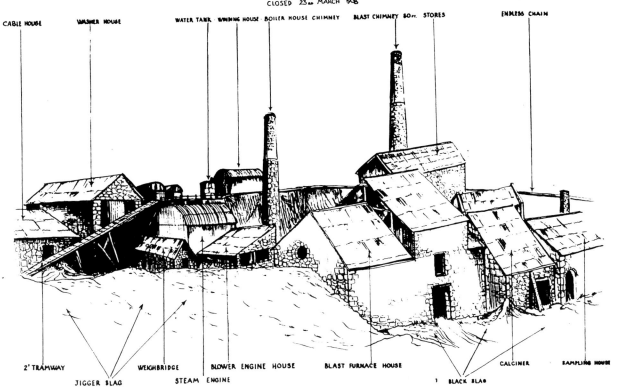

ST. CUTHBERTS LEAD WORKS
PRIDDY, MENDIP HILLS. SOMERSET.
CLOSED 23ᴿᴰ MARCH 1908

CABLE HOUSE   WASHER HOUSE   WATER TANK   WINDING HOUSE   BOILER HOUSE CHIMNEY   BLAST CHIMNEY 80ft   STORES   ENDLESS CHAIN

2' TRAMWAY   WEIGHBRIDGE   BLOWER ENGINE HOUSE   BLAST FURNACE HOUSE   CALCINER   SAMPLING HOUSE

JIGGER SLAG   STEAM ENGINE   BLACK SLAG

63 *Annotated Plan of St Cuthbert's Lead Works, Priddy.*

During the Victorian period the lead industry on Mendip concentrated on the re-smelting of slag left by earlier activity. The re-smelted lead was brittle, containing an appreciable quantity of arsenic, and was especially suitable for making into lead shot. It was transported to Bristol after smelting, where it was processed at the shot tower in Bristol. This re-smelting took place on a large scale at Charterhouse, East Harptree, St Cuthbert's Works at Priddy, and the Waldegrave Works at Chewton Mendip. There are extensive industrial remains at these sites, including settling beds, reservoirs, slag heaps, buddles (circular pits for washing slag), ruined buildings, leats, water-wheel pits, condensation shafts, tracks and tramways. Away from the four main centres of activity, the re-smelting of slag took place on a smaller scale. At Biddlecombe near Wells, a small roofless round building, known as the Buddle House, may have been a small furnace house; another very similar structure is remembered at Priddy. The areas of rough ground created by lead extraction, known locally as gruffy ground, are an important part of the industrial landscape.

Silver extraction was associated with the Mendip lead industry in the Roman and post-medieval periods, but there are no records of silver extractions at other times. In the 19th century, silver extraction took place at Charterhouse, where the remains of the Pattinson silver works can still be found.

Explore the Victorian lead-working remains at Charterhouse, where there is an extensive area of industrial archaeology at Blackmoor Reserve and Velvet Bottom. An easygoing trail has been made there which makes it possible for pushchair and wheelchair users to travel around parts of Blackmoor Reserve and Nether Wood. Leaflets are available at the Charterhouse Centre which tell you more about the area and its history.

COAL-MINING

The local coal measures occur in the north of the Mendip Hills and beyond. Within Mendip District, they lie mainly in the area between Chilcompton and Mells. Coal has been mined here since at least the 13th century. The industry expanded through the later Middle Ages, and by the 1600s there are many references to coal-mining in the Coleford, Ashwick and Stratton area. At first only the uppermost seams were worked, by means of shallow drift mines and bell pits. County maps from the 1500s show 'colepits' in the Nettlebridge valley. The Moorwood, Benter, Stratton Common, Edford, Vobster and Coleford areas of the Nettlebridge valley contain rare and valuable early coal-mining remains.

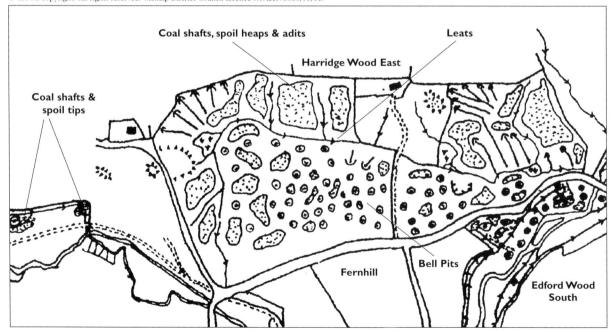

64 *A fascinating and important industrial landscape lies beneath the trees of Harridge Wood East, the record of coal-mining over 600 years or more.*

A 17th century map of coal workings in Coleford shows that, by that date, colliers were mining coal from deep shafts and corridors. The industry gathered pace during the 18th century, an expansion fuelled by an increasing demand for coal for both domestic and industrial use. Improved transport systems, the development of better roads, the Somersetshire Coal Canal, the planned Dorset and Somerset Canal and later the railways, all encouraged the growth of the Mendip coal industry. Coal-mining continued in the Mendip area until 1973.

The archaeology of coal-mining in Mendip encompasses many different types of feature. The colliery sites and buildings, bell pits, shafts, adits, leats, coal tips (locally known as batches), tracks, tramways, inclined planes, railways, canal works, bridges and settlements amount to cultural landscapes of great interest. They are the physical evidence of an activity that had a profound impact on the social and economic development of the area. The sanitising and clearing away of coal-mining landscapes elsewhere in the country means that in Mendip we have probably the best-preserved early coal-mining remains in Britain.

A walk in the Benter and Harridge Wood East areas will take you past some of the earliest coal-mining remains you will find anywhere in Britain.

Other Rural Industries

Peat has been extracted from the low-lying peat moors from at least the Middle Ages, the peat-digging areas being known as turbaries. Its early use was as a fuel, and locally it was used as such well into the Victorian period. The treasurer's accounts for the National Boys' School, Glastonbury, list fuel expenses in 1854 as nine shillings and eight pence for 'coals and turf'. Now it is used only for horticultural purposes.

Stone quarrying is a long-established industry in the area. The diverse geology has contributed to the distinctiveness of Mendip's buildings and settlements, which range from the pink and red sandstones of the Wells area, through the soft greys of lower lias in the Street to Lydford area, and the attractive golden forest marble of the north-eastern part of the district, with many more variations.

The turnpiking of roads in the 18th century created an increasing demand for road stone, a demand that has accelerated ever since. The 20th century has seen an immense growth in the quarrying industry, and the greatest activity has been concentrated in the east Mendip area, with a cluster of large quarries between Frome and Shepton Mallet. Disused 20th century quarries with their quarry faces, ruined buildings, abandoned tools, tracks and tramways are interesting places which have their own historic value.

65 *19th century quarrying tools.*

66 *Peat has been cut on the moors since at least the 13th century.*

67 *Traditionally, peat was cut into blocks which were left to dry before being stacked into tall beehive-shaped 'mumps'.*

68 *The Anglo-Bavarian Brewery, Shepton Mallet.*

The reliability and purity of Mendip water made it a centre for paper-making from at least the 16th century. Paper mills operated at Wookey Hole and nearby at St Cuthbert's Mill, Henley, at Dulcote, Sherborne, and Stoke Bottom. There are buildings, water engineering works, and associated settlements remaining at all these sites.

Textile production was a mainstay of the Mendip economy from the Middle Ages until the 19th century. Wool, silk, velvet, crêpe, moleskin and tweed were all produced, but the area was primarily known for its woollen broadcloths and lighter cloths called Spanish Medleys. Evidence of the physical impact of post-medieval textile production on the landscape is chiefly in the built environment: we still have many of the domestic buildings of cloth workers and clothiers, and a number of industrial buildings such as wool-drying stoves, factory premises and mills. In the wider landscape there are numerous leats, shifted stream and river courses, and millponds related to the textile industry. Mills frequently changed their function to meet the need of the moment, their power being turned to corn grinding, cloth fulling, silk spinning, edge-tool grinding and so on as required.

There were a huge number of mills in Mendip in the 18th and 19th centuries. For example, there is evidence of at least 25 mills along the course of the Mells Stream and its tributaries between Great Elm and Gurney Slade.

Leather-working has a long history in the area, but its main landscape impact and economic importance date from the 19th and 20th centuries when the small village of Street developed into a bustling settlement, with an economy founded on the leather-working and shoe-manufacturing process. At Glastonbury, leather-working and sheepskin processing at the Morland's factory had a strong impact on the local economy and landscape. Minor tanneries existed elsewhere: there are surviving tannery buildings at North Wootton, and at Tannery Farm, Pilton, and the industry was important at Baltonsborough for a time.

Brewing, cider- and perry-making have been important in Mendip's industrial history. Many farmhouses had 18th or 19th century cider houses, most of which have been lost or converted to other uses. Breweries, maltings and other related buildings survive at Shepton Mallet and Frome. At Oakhill, the hamlet owes its character and most of its buildings to the large brewery there. The development of the brewery brought not only a factory, maltings, offices and warehouses, but also chapels, workers' and managers' houses, stables for the dray-horses, water supplies and the only brewery light railway in England.

Wanstrow was the centre of a post-medieval pottery industry, producing attractive glazed earthenware vessels and dishes. Very little research has been undertaken as yet, but the clay pits, kilns and waste heaps of the industry are important evidence of this phase of activity.

Iron-working and edge-tool production were important in the east Mendip area in the 18th and 19th centuries. The area's best-known example of an iron-working site is Fussell's edge-tool works in the Wadbury Valley near Mells. There are extensive remains at the remote abandoned riverside location, which is east Mendip's best-loved archaeological site, fascinating to experts and the general public alike.

There were six Fussell's ironworks in the area - two at Mells, one each at Great Elm, Railford, Chantry and Nunney. Other iron-working landscape features include the abandoned iron pits near Higher Pits Farm, Priddy, and the engineered roadway used by the Mendip Haematite Company to bring their ore down from the Mendip plateau into Wookey Hole. An area of substantial earthworks and slag heaps at Henley near Wookey marks the place where an iron mill stood by the early 17th century

A walk down the Wadbury Valley between Mells and Great Elm takes you past the fascinating ruins of Fussell's Ironworks, once a thriving edge-tool works.

WORLD WAR II DEFENCES

Mendip has an impressive array of World War II defences, ranging from pill-boxes and anti-tank trenches to the important decoy town constructed on Black Down. The pill-boxes were augmented by objects designed to obstruct the progress of enemy troops. These were colloquially known as dragon's teeth: many were simply large concrete cubes, but in the Wellow valley area a pyramid shape was used. Mendip's pill-boxes and defensive obstructions were not randomly placed in the landscape, but formed one of a number of strategic stop lines in the south-west of England. The angular lines of a deep anti-tank trench running close to Maesbury Camp can be seen on 1940s RAF aerial photographs. Most of these features were filled in many years ago, but the present field boundary to the east of the hillfort is a rare surviving fragment. On Black Down you can see curious heather-covered humps set out in regular lines on the hill top; they were meant to mislead enemy bombers into dropping their bombs early during raids on Bristol.

69 *This World War II anti-tank defence at Dinder is part of a strategic defence line across Somerset.*

CHAPTER 9

CARING FOR MENDIP'S PAST

This book has explored the way that our present landscape has developed over thousands of years of human activity. We live with an extraordinary time-depth in the everyday world about us - any walk or drive through Mendip takes you past sites and features of widely ranging dates. It is a wonderful but vulnerable resource, which will need care and conservation if it is to survive to give pleasure and knowledge to future generations. Although various authorities (Mendip District Council, Somerset County Council, English Heritage and others) can help in this task, ultimately the welfare of historic sites, features and buildings depends upon the local community.

It is important that people feel a personal sense of commitment and responsibility, and that they take positive steps to care for local historic features. Listed below are some ways in which individuals and communities can improve the survival chances of local heritage resources.

How can I help?

• Undertake practical conservation projects, for example, consolidating buildings and structures in need of repair. Examples of similar recent projects have been the removal of ivy from a disused railway at Buckland Dinham, the clearance of shrubs from Murtry aqueduct, the re-roofing of Pilton Tithe Barn. It is, of course, essential to obtain help and guidance before embarking on work of this kind.

• Carry out historic landscape surveys, recording features and researching the history of an area. Recent examples include research into coal-mining remains in the Nettlebridge Valley, the Downhead Historic Landscape Survey, and the Defence of Britain project which recorded World War II defences.

• Avoid unnecessary 'tidying up' of humps and bumps and ruins in the countryside, for example small quarry pits, areas of uneven ground, old limekilns, former mill leats, former cottage sites, etc.

• Avoid destroying or damaging archaeological sites. While it is easy to see that levelling sites is damaging, it is often not appreciated that removing archaeological evidence from them is also very harmful. The systematic collection of flints by collectors, or the looting of sites by metal detectorists is strongly discouraged.

• Try to maintain the present character of a building, settlement or area of countryside. Some of this work, of course, comes under the planning process, but much

relies only upon the sensitivity and goodwill of farmers and property owners. For example, maintain existing stone walls and other boundaries, restore and renovate buildings and structures where this is appropriate, and, health and safety permitting, avoid demolishing ruins.

• The use of traditional building and repair skills is encouraged; further information is available from Mendip District Council's Conservation Section.

Both Mendip District Council and Somerset County Council are happy to give help and advice on historic environment conservation projects, and would like to be kept informed of the findings of research projects. If you would like to find out what sites and features are already known for your study area, please contact the Sites and Monuments Register Officer at Somerset County Council. The Somerset Studies Library, Paul Street, Taunton has an excellent collection of Ordnance Survey maps, illustrations and books, while the County Record Office at Obridge Road, Taunton is the place to look for tithe and estate maps and documents.

You may like to join a historical or archaeological group or a local museum society. In Mendip there are a number of keen groups, including those based at Oakhill, Evercreech, Wells, Pilton, Frome, Glastonbury, Strode College and Shepton Mallet. The Somerset Archaeological and Natural History Society is highly recommended for many reasons, including its fine library, excellent annual publication and good meetings programme.

While encouraging an active interest in the historic landscape, we are keen that you should act carefully and responsibly. Take care not to trespass - if you decide to visit a site or to undertake your own research, be sure to obtain the landowner's permission. Do not dig into or attempt to excavate sites - archaeological sites are vulnerable, and irreplaceable information can be destroyed in this way. The conservation ethic now governs our management of archaeological sites - they should not be excavated without very good reason, and only then under expert guidance. If you discover a previously unknown site, then contact either the archaeological team at Somerset County Council or the Countryside Officer at Mendip District Council. There is new legislation concerning the reporting of some archaeological material, particularly metalwork. Information about the Portable Antiquities Regulations can be obtained from the County Museum Service at Taunton Castle.

The landscape is dynamic, change has always occurred and will continue, but with care and effort we can minimise the loss of historic value from our settlements and countryside, so that as much as possible of Mendip's rich heritage is handed on to future generations in good condition.

Useful addresses:

Penny Stokes, Countryside heritage, archaeology and local museums in Mendip, Mendip District Council, Cannards Grave Road, Shepton Mallet BA4 5BT. Tel: 01749 343399 Website: www.mendip.gov.uk

Bob Croft, Environment and Property Dept., Archaeology and records of listed buildings in Somerset, Somerset County Council, County Hall, Taunton TA1 4DY. Tel: 01823 356089

David Dawson, County Museums Service, Somerset County Council, County Hall, Taunton TA1 4DY. Tel: 01823 356089

Sarah Jackson, Mendip Hills AONB Officer, Charterhouse Centre, Nr Blagdon, Bristol BS18 6XR. Tel: 01761 463357

70 *This small limekiln at Thrupe, Croscombe, is a rare survivor of 18th century enclosure activity.*

71 *The medieval barn at Pilton is soon to be re-roofed.*

FURTHER READING

The following is a list of books and published articles relevant to the Mendip area. It is not exhaustive and readers undertaking a study are encouraged to seek out other material from the local history section at the public libraries and from the Somerset Studies section at the central library in Taunton. The library of the Somerset Archaeological and Natural History Society is housed with the Somerset Studies collection, and non-members are permitted to consult it, although not to borrow from it. There are many useful notes, articles and references to be found in the published proceedings of the University of Bristol Speleological Society and the Somerset Archaeological and Natural History Society, abbreviated below to *PUBSS* and *PSANHS* respectively.

MULTI-PERIOD

Adkins, L. & Adkins, R., 1992. *A Field Guide to Somerset Archaeology*
Atthill, R., ed., 1976. *Mendip: A New Study*
Aston, M. & Burrow, I., 1982. *The Archaeology of Somerset*
Aston, M. et al., ongoing series. *The Shapwick Project Annual Reports*
Barrington, N. & Stanton, W., 1976. *Mendip: The Complete Caves and a View of the Hills*
Collinson, J., 1791. *The History and Antiquities of the County of Somerset*
Coysh, A.W., Mason, E.J. & Waite, V., 1954. *The Mendips*
Croft, R. & Aston, M., 1993. *Somerset from the Air*
Dobson, D.P., 1931. *The Archaeology of Somerset*
Ellis, P., 1992. *Mendip Hills: An Archaeological Survey of the Area of Outstanding Natural Beauty*
Gough, J., 1930. *The Mines of Mendip*
Hall, W.G., ed., n.d. *Man and the Mendips*
Phelps, W., 1836. *History and Antiquities of Somersetshire*
Thomas, G.A.P. & Jones, G.D.B., 1978. 'The East Somerset Survey, 1975-1977', *Aerial Archaeology* 2, 68-70
Todd, M., 1993. 'Charterhouse on Mendip: An Interim Report on Survey and Excavation in 1993', *PSANHS* 137, 59-68
Todd, M., 1995. 'Charterhouse on Mendip: An Interim Report on Excavations in 1994', *PSANHS* 138, 75-80
Victoria County Histories
Williams, M, 1970. *The Draining of the Somerset Levels*
Williams, R., 1989. 'Smeatham's Batch: A Mendip Barrow, Spoilheap or Boundary Cairn', *Bristol and Avon Archaeology* 8, 51-2

FOR THE PREHISTORIC AND ROMAN PERIODS

Ashworth, H.W.W., 1970. *Report on the Roman-British Settlement and Metallurgical Workings at Vespasian Farm, Green Ore, Wells*
Avery, M., 1968. 'Excavations at Meare East, 1966', in *PSANHS* 112 (1968), 21-39
Balch, H.E., 1912. 'Further Excavations at the Late Celtic and Romano-British Cave-dwelling at Wookey Hole, Somerset', *Archaeologia* 44 (1912), 337-46
Balch, H.E., 1914, *Wookey Hole: Its Caves and Cave Dwellers*
Balch, H.E., 1928. 'Excavations at Wookey Hole and Other Mendip Caves, 1926-7', *Journal of Antiq.* 8 (1928), 193-210
Balch, H.E. & Troup, R.D.R., 1911. 'A Late Celtic and Romano-British Cave-dwelling at Wookey Hole near Wells, Somerset', *Archaeologia* 43 (1911), 563-92
Barrett, J.H., 1965. 'Tom Tivey's Hole Rock Shelter, near Leighton, Somerset', *PUBSS* 2 (1965), 9-24
Bishop, M., 1974. 'A Preliminary Report on the Middle Pleistocene Mammal Bearing Deposit of Westbury-sub-Mendip, Somerset', *PUBSS* 13 (1974), 302-18
Bishop, M., 1975. 'Earliest Record of Man's Presence in Britain', *Nature* 253 (1975), 95-7
Boon, G.C., 1972. 'Counterfeitors on Mendip', *PUBSS* 13 (1), 70-82
Boyd Dawkins, W., 'Early Man' in *Victoria County History of Somerset*, 167-206
Branigan, K. & Fowler, P.J., 1976. *The Roman West Country: Classical Culture and Celtic Society*
Branigan, K. & Dearne, M.J., 1990. 'The Romano-British Finds from Wookey Hole: A Re-appraisal', *PSANHS* 134, 57-80
Budge, A.R., Russell, J.R. & Boon, G.C., 1974. 'Excavations and Fieldwork at Charterhouse-on-Mendip, 1960-67', *PUBSS* 13 (13), 327-47
BUFAU, 1990. *Romans in Shepton Mallet: Excavations at Fosse Lane, 1990*
Bulleid, A., 1926. *The Lake Villages of Somerset*
Bulleid, A., 1933. 'Ancient Trackway in Meare Heath, Somerset', *PSANHS* 79, 19-20
Bulleid, A. & Gray, H. St G., 1911 & 1917. *The Glastonbury Lake Village*, Vols. 1 and 2
Bulleid, A. & Gray, H. St G., 1948. *The Meare Lake Village*, Vol. 1
Burrow, E.J., 1924. *Ancient Earthworks and Camps of Somerset*
Burrow, I.C.G., 1981. 'Hillfort and Hill-Top Settlement in Somerset in the First Millennium AD', *British Archaeological Report* 91
Campbell, J.B., Elkington, D., Fowler, P. & Grinsell, L.V., 1970. *The Mendip Hills in Prehistoric and Roman Times*
Coles, J.M. & Orme, B.J., 1980. *Prehistory of the Somerset Levels*
Coles, J.M. & Coles B., 1986. *Sweet Track to Glastonbury: The Somerset Levels in Prehistory*
Coles, J.M. & Minnitt, S., 1997. *Industrious and Fairly Civilized: Glastonbury Lake Village*
Corcoran, J.X.W.P., 1954. 'The Iron Handle and Bronze Bands from Read's Cavern: A Reinterpretation', *PUBSS* 7, 46-50
Gray, H. St G., 1905. 'Excavations at Small Down Camp near Evercreech, 1904', *PSANHS* 50, 32-49
Gray, H. St G., 1908. 'Maesbury Camp or Maesbury Castle', *PSANHS* 53, 73-81
Gray, H. St G., 1910. 'Excavations at the Amphitheatre, Charterhouse-on-Mendip, 1909', *PSAHNS* 55, 118-37
Gray, H. St G., 1930. 'Excavation at Kings Down Camp, Mells, Somerset, 1927-9', *Archaeologia* 80, 59-98
Gray, H. St G. & Bulleid, A., 1953. *The Meare Lake Village*, Vol. 2
Grinsell, L.V., 1969. 'Somerset Barrows, Part I: West and South', *PSANHS* 113, 1-43
Grinsell, L.V., 1969. 'Somerset Barrows, Part II: North and East', *PSANHS* 115, 44-137
Hawkes, C.J., Rogers, J.M. & Tratman, E.K., 1978. 'Romano-British Cemetery in the Fourth Chamber of Wookey Hole Cave, Somerset', *PUBSS* 15 (1), 23-52
Jacobi, R., 1982. 'The Environment of Man at Cheddar: 11-10,000 Years Ago', *PSANHS* 126, 1-16
Langford, F., 1922. 'Third Report on Read's Cavern', *PUBSS* 1, 135-43
Langford, F., 1923. 'Fourth Report on Read's Cavern', *PUBSS* 2, 51-8
Leach, P., 1990. 'The Roman Site at Fosse Lane, Shepton Mallet', *PSANHS* 134, 47-56
Leach, P., 1991. *Shepton Mallet: Romano-Britons & Early Christians in Somerset*

Leech, R., 1977. *Romano-British Rural Settlement in South Somerset and North Dorset*, unpublished thesis, University of Bristol

Leech, R., 1986. 'The Excavation of a Romano-Britsh Temple and Later Cemetery on Lamyatt Beacon, Somerset', *Britannia* 17, 259-329

Levitan, B. et al, 1988. 'Charterhouse Warren Farm Swallet, Mendip, Somerset', *PUBSS* 18 (2), 171-239

McDonnell, R., 1979. 'The Upper Axe Valley: An Interim Statement', *PSANHS* 123, 75-82

Overend, E., 1962. 'Aerial Photographs of the Frome Area', *PSANHS* 106, 77-80

Palmer, L.S., 1920. 'The Keltic Cavern', *PUBSS* 1 (1919-20), 9-20

Palmer, L.S., 1921. 'The Keltic Cavern', *PUBSS* 1 (1920-21), 87-91

Palmer, L.S. & Ashworth, H.W.W., 1957. 'Four Roman Pigs of Lead from the Mendips', *PSANHS* 101, 52-88

Peacock, D.P.S., 1969, 'A Contribution to the Study of Glastonbury Ware from South-Western Britain', *Antiquity* 43 (1969), 145-9

Read, R.F., 1924. 'Second Report on the Excavation of the Mendip Barrows', *PUBSS* 2 (2), 136-46

Stanton, W., 1986. 'Natural Sinkholes Affecting the Priddy Circles', *PUBSS* 17 (3), 353-8

Taylor, C. & Tratman, E. K., 1957. 'The Priddy Circles: Preliminary Report', *PUBSS* 8 (1), 7-17

The Somerset Levels Papers, a series of annual reports beginning in 1975

Tratman, E.K., 1924. 'Fifth Report on Read's Cavern', *PUBSS* 2 (1924), 125-7

Tratman, E.K., 1931. 'Read's Cavern: Final Report', *PUBSS* 4 (1931), 8-10

Tratman, E.K., 1959. 'Maesbury Castle, Somerset', *PUBSS* 8 (1959), 171-8

Tratman, E.K., 1967. 'The Priddy Circles, Mendip, Somerset: Henge Monuments', *PUBSS* 11 (1) (1967), 97-125

Tratman, E.K., 1970. 'The Glastonbury Lake Village: A Reconsideration', *PUBSS* 12 (1970), 143-67

Tratman, E.K., 1975. 'The Cave Archaeology and Palaeontology of Mendip', in Smith, D.I., ed, *Limestone and Caves of the Mendip Hills*, 352-91

Tratman, E.K., Donovan, D.T. & Campbell, J.B., 1971. 'The Hyaena Den (Wookey Hole), Mendip Hills, Somerset', *PUBSS* 12 (3) (1924), 245-79

FOR THE SAXON AND MEDIEVAL PERIODS

Abrams, L. & Carley, J.P., eds., 1991. *The Archaeology and History of Glastonbury Abbey*

Abrams, L., 1996. *Anglo-Saxon Glastonbury: Church and Endowment*

Aston, M., ed., 1988. *Aspects of the Medieval Landscape of Somerset*

Aston, M. & Lewis, C., 1994. *The Medieval Landscape of Wessex*

Bond, J. & Weller, J.B., 1991. 'The Somerset Barns of Glastonbury Abbey' in Abrams & Carley, 1991.

Burrow, I. & Burrow, C., 1990. 'Witham Priory: The First English Carthusian Monastery', *PSANHS* 134, 141-82

Carley, J.P., 1985. *Glastonbury Abbey: The Holy House at the Head of the Moors Adventurous*

Church, C., 1894. *Chapters in the Early History of the Church of Wells*

Costen, M., 1992. *The Origins of Somerset*

Darby, H.C. & Finn, R.W., 1967. *The Domesday Geography of South West England*

Edwards, H., 1988. *The Charters of the Early West Saxon Kingdom*

Finberg, H.P. R., 1964 . *The Early Charters of Wessex*

Garmonsway, G.N., 1954. *The Anglo-Saxon Chronicle*

Grundy, G.B., 1935. *The Saxon Charters and Field Names of Somerset*

Haslam, J., 1984. *Anglo-Saxon Towns in Southern England*

Hollinrake, C. & Hollinrake, N., 1991. 'A Late Saxon Monastic Enclosure Ditch and Canal, Glastonbury, Somerset', *Antiquity* 65, 117-8

Hollinrake, C. & Hollinrake, N., 1992. 'The Abbey Enclosure Ditch and a Late-Saxon Canal: Rescue Excavations at Glastonbury, 1984-88', *PSANHS* 136, 73-94

McGarvie, M., 1979. *The Bounds of Selwood*

Morland, S., 1990. 'The Somerset Hundreds in the Geld Inquest and their Domesday Manors', *PSANHS* 134, 95-140

Pattison, P., 1991. 'Settlement and Landscape at Ramspits, Deerleap, Westbury-Sub-Mendip', *PSANHS* 135, 95-106

Pooley, C., 1877. *An Historical and Descriptive Account of the Old Stone Crosses of Somerset*

Radford, C.A.R., 1963. 'The Church in Somerset down to 1100', *PSANHS* 106, 28-45

Radford, C.A.R., 1981. 'Glastonbury Abbey before 1184: Interim Report of the Excavations, 1908-64', in *Medieval Art and Architecture at Wells Cathedral*, British Archaeological Association Conference Transactions 4 (1981), 110-34

Rahtz, P.A., 1964. 'Excavations at Chalice Well, Glastonbury', *PSANHS* 108, 145-63

Rahtz, P.A., 1971. 'Excavations on Glastonbury Tor', *Archaeological Journal* 127, 1-81

Rahtz, P.A., 1974. 'Pottery in Somerset AD400-1066', in Evison et al., *Medieval Pottery from Excavations* (1974), 95-126

Rahtz, P.A., 1976. 'Irish Settlements in Somerset', *Proceedings of the Royal Irish Academy* 76, Section C, 223-30

Rahtz, P.A. & Hirst, S.M., 1974. *Beckery Chapel, Glastonbury, 1967-8*

Rahtz, P.A., 1993. *Glastonbury*

Rigold, S.E., 1957. *Nunney Castle, Somerset*

Rodwell, W., 1979. *Wells Cathedral: Excavations and Discoveries*

Rodwell, W., 1980. 'Wells, the Cathedral and City', *Current Archaeology* 73, 38-44

Rodwell, W., 1981. 'The Lady Chapel by the Cloister at Wells and the Site of the Anglo-Saxon Cathedral', in *Medieval Art and Architecture at Wells Cathedral*, British Archaeological Association Conference Transactions 4, 1-9

Sawyer, P., 1968. *Anglo-Saxon Charters*

Scrase, A., 1983. *Wells: A Study in Town Origins*

Scrase, A., 1989. 'A French Merchant in Fourteenth Century Wells', *PSANHS,* 131-40

Shaw, D., 1993. *The Creation of a Community: The City of Wells in the Middle Ages*

Thompson, E.M., 1895. *The Somerset Carthusians*

Thorn, C. & Thorn, F., 1980. *Domesday Book: 8, Somerset*

Wilcox, R.J.A., 1980. 'Excavations at Farleigh Hungerford Castle, Somerset, 1973-76', *PSANHS* 124, 87-109

Williams, E.H.D., et al., 1986. 'New Street, Mells', *PSANHS* 130, 115-26

Woods, H., 1995. 'Excavations at Glastonbury Abbey, 1987-1993', *PSANHS* 138, 7-74

For printed versions of medieval documents

Elton, C.I., ed., 1891. *Rentalia and Custumaria of Glastonbury Abbey*

Historical Manuscripts Commission, 1907 & 1914. *Calendar of the Manuscripts of the Dean and Chapter of Wells*

Jackson, J.E., ed., 1882. *Liber Henrici de Soliaco Abbatis Glaston*

Watkin, A., 1944, 1948, 1949-50. *The Glastonbury Chartulary*

FOR BOTH MEDIEVAL AND POST-MEDIEVAL PERIODS

Armstrong, K., 1997. *Croscombe: The History of a Village*

Aston, M.A. & Leech, R.H., 1977. *Historic Towns in Somerset: Archaeology and Planning*

Belham, P., 1973. *The Making of Frome*

Belham, P., 1992. *Villages of the Frome Area: A History*

Cleverdon, F.W., 1974. *A History of Mells*

Cocke, T., Findlay, D., Halsey, R. & Williamson, E., 1989. *Recording a Church: An Illustrated Glossary* (CBA Practical Handbook)

Colt Hoare, R., 1824. *Monastic Remains of the Religious Houses at Witham, Bruton & Stavordale, Somerset*

Dunning, R.W., 1976. *Christianity in Somerset*

Dunning, R.W., 1978. *History of Somerset*

Dunning, R.W., 1994. *Glastonbury*

Farbrother, J.E., 1860. *Shepton Mallet*

Good, G.L. & Russett, V.E.J., 1987. 'Common Types of Earthenware Found in the Bristol Area', *Bristol and Avon Archaeology* 6, 35-43

Gough, J.W., 1966. *Mendip Mining Laws and Forest Bounds*

Hasler, J. & Luker, B., 1993. 'The Site of the Bishop's Palace, Wookey', *PSANHS* 137, 111-18

Hasler, J. & Luker, B., 1993. 'An Industrial Site at Wookey', *PSANHS* 137, 119-22

Hasler, J. & Luker, B., 1997. *The Parish of Wookey: A New History*

McGarvie, M., 1980. *The Book of Frome*

McGarvie, M., 1989. *Witham Friary Church and Parish*

McGarvie, M., 1990. *The Book of Street*

Parsons, D., 1989. *Churches and Chapels: Investigating Places of Worship* (CBA Practical Handbook)

Pevsner, N., 1958. *The Buildings of England: North Somerset and Bristol*

Ponting, K.G., 1971. *The Woollen Industry of South-West England*

Ponting, K.G., 1975. *Wool and Water*

Reid, R.D., 1979. *Some Buildings of Mendip*

Rogers, K., 1976. *Wiltshire and Somerset Woollen Mills*

Seal, J., 1993. *Doulting: The History of a Somerset Village*

SSAVBRG, 1988. *The Vernacular Buildings of Batcombe*

Williams, M., 1970. *The Draining of the Somerset Levels*

Wilson-North, R., 1997. 'Witham from Carthusian Monastery to Country House', *Current Archaeology* 148

Windrum, A., 1998. *The History of Nunney*

FOR THE POST-MEDIEVAL PERIOD

Atthill, R., 1964, 1971. *Old Mendip* (1st, 2nd eds.)

Atthill, R., 1967. *The Somerset and Dorset Railway*

Bentley, J. & Murless, B., 1985. *Somerset Roads: Legacy of the Turnpikes*

Billingsley, J., 1798. *A General View of the Agriculture of the County of Somerset*

Clew, K., 1971. *The Dorset and Somerset Canal: An Illustrated History*

Collier P. & Skene, D., 1986. *Colliers' Way*

Coombs, H. & Bax, A.M., eds., 1971. *Journal of a Somerset Rector, 1803-1834: John Skinner, A.M., Antiquary, 1772-1839*

Davis, F., n.d. *The Anglo*

Davis, F., *A Shepton Mallet Camera*, Vols. 1-5

De Viggiani, M., 1985. *A Cranmore Chronicle*

De Viggiani, M., 1988. *Two Estates: The Story of an East Mendip Village*

Down, C.G. & Warrington, A.J., n.d. *The History of the Somerset Coalfield*

Greenwood, C. & J., 1822. *Somerset Delineated*

Kelly's Directory of Somerset

Hawkins, M., 1988. *Somerset at War, 1939-1945*

Hylton, Lord, 1910. *Notes on the History of the Parish of Kilmersdon*

Leech, R., 1981. *Early Industrial Housing: The Trinity Area of Frome*

Maggs, C. G., 1991. *The Last Years of the Somerset and Dorset*

McGarvie, M., 1974. 'Marston House: A Study of Its History and Architecture', *PSANHS* 118, 15-24

Munckton, T., 1996. *Chancellors Farm Accounts, 1766-1767*

Strawbridge, D., 1990. *Meandering through Chilcompton*

Tate, W.E., 1948. *Somerset Enclosure Acts and Awards*

Tratman, E.K., 1966. 'Decoy Mounds on Blackdown, Mendip', *PUBSS* 11 (1), 44

Williams, M., 1971. 'The Enclosure and Reclamation of the Mendip Hills, 1770-1870', *The Agricultural History Review* 19, Pt 1, 65-80

Williams, M., 1972. 'The Enclosure of Waste Land in Somerset, 1700-1900', *Transactions of the Institute of British Geographers*

THINGS WE VALUE

'As to our views on heritage in this parish, we leave it to others to praise the medieval church of St Matthew, the Victorian simplicity of Christ Church, Henton, the nationally recognised site of the Bishop's palace in Wookey, the eccentricity of the 18th century Mellifont (so-called) Abbey. We would like to record the less obvious items: the huddled cottages of the settlements; the old farmhouses like Yew Tree in Wookey, Cross Farm at Yarley and Double House in Henton; the mills dating back to at least the 13th century at Burcott and at Bleadney; in connection with the mills, the second largest man-made item in the parish, the millstream running beside the B3139; and finally, the largest of all, and the most important, the landscape itself, shaped over thousands of years and still being shaped today.'

B. G. Luker, Chairman, Wookey Parish Council

'East Pennard village Conservation Area is particularly valued for its important unspoilt representation of a late 18th and 19th century estate village superimposed and to a great extent conditioned by the still discernible medieval landscape framework. In addition to the full complement of vernacular buildings, ecclesiastical, secular, domestic and agricultural, there are many important minor features such as the flagged paths and the unique survival of two paved paths created to prevent fouling of gentry footwear by muddy roads, as well as garden features, railings, evergreen hedges and walls. The relationship of buildings to their landscape setting and process of evolution is seen as particularly important, and is often in danger of neglect. Throughout the parish remain many fine vernacular farmhouses and cottages from all periods, including a rare cob survival of what must have been a predominant material. Many Victorian farm buildings also survive, though are threatened by regrettable 'barn conversions'. The landscape retains a wooded appearance thanks to the remaining hedgerow density and surviving green lanes, though further loss of hedgerows and traditional orchards is an ever present threat. Ridge and furrow and other earthworks are at risk, especially by maize cultivation. The specimen trees and plantings around the village add greatly to its value and are an integral part of its evolutionary process.

'Some areas of the parish have by the creeping suburbanisation of building technique and design lost much of their original character, which can only be maintained by use of local materials and styles. Archaeologically important areas and surviving earthworks need to be recognised so that even if not scheduled they can be considered as important aspects in landscape policy.'

Adrian Pearse for East Pennard Parish Council

'Distinctive area features e.g. church towers. Local designs of gate latches, gate styles. Place-names such as Shepton Mallet, and historic events connected with local places.'

Anon.

In the Shepton Mallet area: 'The high stone walls, the pedestrian walkways, Church Lane, the church, Collett Park, footpaths, Barren Down (this name must surely be a corruption of Barrow Down). The historic buildings in general.'

Retired Medical Secretary and GP

In the West Horrington area: 'The buddle house of Biddlecombe, Horrington Hill, Horrington Wood, hedges, stone walls, streams. Greater emphasis must be given to the status of Areas of Outstanding Natural Beauty. There are far too many transgressions of the current criteria to make them truly effective.'

Ken Russell, St Cuthbert Out

'The way of life in which people lived and farmed with nature and valued the seasons for what they gave to them. Today it seems that we try to go against nature, to the cost of the planet.'

Mr and Mrs M. Cole, retired, keen walkers, Ashcott

In the Shepton Mallet area: 'The archaeological value of the Fosse Lane area and its importance in the development of the area. Beacon Hill and its barrows. The Fosse Road and its hedgerows, stone stiles, dew ponds (that are gradually disappearing). Stone walls that are a feature of Shepton Mallet and dry-stone walls wherever they exist in the countryside around the town. Listed buildings at risk. The surrounding landscape (particularly at Charlton) that is likely to be swallowed up by several hundred houses. Collett Park.'

Fred Davis, Chairman, Shepton Mallet Museum Society and Beacon Society

'Farms where hedgerow trees such as oak and ash are retained and new young trees encouraged to develop; the local character of traditional orchards; the old trackways and droves (without motorcycle access); old cast iron finger post signs; encouragement for old barns to be maintained and not necessarily converted to housing.'

John and Ruth Rawlings, Baltonsborough

'The old stone stiles and gateposts of Mendip, some of Doulting and Dulcote stone. Also in the Priddy area gate posts of stone from the Draycott and Rodney Stoke quarries.'

Jane Linthorne, housewife and librarian, Stoke St Michael

'The historic heritage of the village of Kilmersdon is greatly valued by the school and makes a significant contribution to the education and experiences planned for pupils attending the school. The range of buildings in the village, the local sights of natural beauty, the calm and tranquil surroundings, the famed Jack and Jill Hill and a large number of local people who are willing to share their memories with pupils are all used by the staff to generate real experiences that capture children's interest and imagination, particularly in the areas of History, Geography and English. Panoramic views from the school, and the atmosphere and mood of the surrounding countryside at different points of the year stimulate and support Art, Music and Religious Education.

'Buildings and sites which are of particular value include the parish church, the Old Schoolhouse, the Old Post Office, the Manor House, Tumblers Bottom, the Jolliffe Arms, the Village Hall, Coles Garden, the wide variety of housing in the village, the variation in age of property in the village, the Ammerdown estate, Babington Woods, the physical features of the land surrounding the school, Jack and Jill Hill and the well that stands in the school grounds, the villages of Holcombe, Chilcompton, Mells and the surrounding quarrying communities.'

Sue Heal, Kilmersdon C. of E. (V.A.) Primary School

In the Rode area: 'The old stone cottages and houses - especially those looking onto the Green. The pumps in Lower Street, preserved but not in working order, sadly. The Big and Little Shard, the flagstone pavement along the west side of the Green, the wonderful variations of height and shape of the roofs between Lower Street and the High Street as the buildings clamber up the hill there. Seen from the top of Walnut Close these are really a special view. In Tellisford, the bridge and steps, in Rode Scutts Bridge and its medieval associations.'

Retired resident of Rode, Tellisford and Woolverton

'Encourage landowners, tenants and farmers to know and care about their own historical and archaeological features. Old roads and holloways - encourage farmers not to fill them in; signposts - keep the unique Somerset triangular top, replace broken arms with traditional cast iron type.

'Milestones and mile posts - get the Highways Department to look after them and paint them; pounds; non-highway bridges over minor streams; stone stiles; sluices and water meadows; water mills and leats; stone walls - give grants for rebuilding; lime-kilns, hydraulic rams, dovecotes; hedges, boundary stones, canals, railways, small quarries, bullpits, windmill sites; earthworks in fields - do not allow them to be ploughed out; stone pavements - in Norton St Philip these are very important, no more paviours or tarmac replacements.'

Colin Brett, semi-retired chemist more keen on the past than the future!, Norton St Philip

'Old buildings of any type but particularly masonry-built, for example, Murtry Bridge, Murtry Aqueduct, the Via Crucis at St John's Frome; items having relevance to Frome's history, for example Thomas Bunn's grave; old industrial sites, like Fussell's Ironworks, abandoned quarries containing old machinery or ironwork, tramways etc.'

Deryck Ingram, Frome

'The peace and tranquility of Charterhouse. It would be wonderful to have public access to the settlement and amphitheatre areas at times. I wish the Mendips to remain peaceful.'

Mrs Claydon, retired SRN

In the Oakhill area: 'The special landscape around the village - as you approach it is obvious that trees dominate the village, as its name implies. There are also areas of woodland such as Beacon Wood, Home and Harridge Woods. Also the Iron Age fort at Maesbury; the Roman Fosse Way discernible in fields; the ancient parish church of St James, Ashwick, the Victorian All Saints Church at Oakhill, and the Methodist Chapel built in 1825; the site and ruins of Ashwick Grove House which was the home of the noted 18th century agriculturalist John Billingsley.'

Mr J. Gilling, Ashwick

In the Coleford area: 'The very fine network of public footpaths, many of which are themselves historic (e.g. the towpaths of the abandoned Dorset and Somerset Canal); the aqueduct in Coleford is still standing but desperately in need of attention as are the few remaining coke ovens at Vobster; the remains of the Mackintosh Mine; the site of a Knight's Templar settlement in Newbury. The lost village of Fernhill at Stoke Bottom, which still has the walls of dwellings standing with living spaces visible; they line the village street which is still intact. The valley of the Mells Stream is very beautiful and contains precious areas of ancient woodland and some fields that have been farmed sympathetically and therefore exhibit a wealth of wild flowers, birds and butterflies.'

David Higgs, Hon. Sec. Coleford Millennium Project

'Fussell's Ironworks, Vallis Vale in general, the Mendip Hills'.

Bob Caudwell, retired, amateur photographer, Frome

'What has been done in the Tor area (despite the mindless vandalism at times) to preserve the habitat and our heritage. Would like to see road signs reading 'Slow Native Animals Crossing!'. We live in a special place: we must remember to appreciate it and to share it with others, especially the young.'

Bryn Whitcombe, Rainbow Warrior, Glastonbury

'Our green areas. In particular the Tor (which deserves Ancient Monument status) Bushy Coombe, Wearyall Hill, Fishers Hill, the Abbey Grounds, and St Bride's Mound.' [Comments and ideas regarding the management of these places were included.]

John Brunsdon, Glastonbury Town Council

In the Glastonbury area: 'Sacred sites, whether to Celtic deities which cannot be archaeologically proved, or later Christian (often on old sacred spots). I am concerned about development creeping closer, and onto these sites. I am also concerned about any suggestion of fencing off these sites. All these places should be freely available to us and our children whether for prayer, teaching or just enjoying nature. We value these places free, not interfered with.'

Mrs Burrows, woman, mother, Glastonbury

'Remnants of Somerset Coalfields; canals and old unused railway tracks; the local footpaths and tracks; the unspoilt woodland and animal life; the old churches and historic towns; museums and libraries.'

Richard Wilshen, Coleford

'Hedgerows and walls, with or without history; obviously ancient boundaries; settlements; copses and wildlife.'

Peter Reakes, electrician, and family, Cranmore

'All the old things in the parish, the list is long, but must include the Nettlebridge Valley with its mining past, stone stiles, old buildings and ruins, e.g. Lapwing Farm and Ashwick Grove, holloways, old roads, dewponds, deserted sites, old mill sites, the former Oakhill Brewery Railway (the only brewery in the country to have its own light railway). I could go on and on. I want to photograph and record these things before they disappear for ever.'

Percy Lambert, retired legal cashier and budding local historian, Ashwick

In the Chilcompton area: 'Stone slab stiles; staddle stones; boundary stones; gateposts; bridges, wartime pillboxes and tank trap; trees and stands of trees; vistas and views; footpaths; geological features; the old railway station; former watercress beds; New Rock Colliery; the old pound wall; Blackers Hill fort; a 17th century piped spring water system; bridges; withy beds; the coat of arms on the recreation field wall, and much more.'

David Strawbridge, author and local historian, Chilcompton

'The Roman amphitheatre and fort at Charterhouse; dew ponds, animal dipping areas, lime-kilns, ochre pits. We are very concerned about the apparent lack of legal protection for many historic sites and artefacts in Mendip.'

Elaine and Roger Cookman, former school teacher and chartered surveyor, Wells

'Hedgerows; footpaths; street furniture; chimney pots and cowls; varied street names; pub signs (except when changed without good reason); trig points and bench marks; churchyards; tombstones and memorials; lych gates; sundials.'

R. and J. Mackenzie, Wells

'Nunney Castle. It is essential to leave the village as it is, particularly the Conservation Area, but all older buildings need protection.'

Anthony Windrum, local historian, Nunney

'Fussell's Ironworks are of great historical value; listed buildings; Ammerdown tower; Turner's tower; old mine sites; old routes.'

Mr Robinson, Hemington

'Archaeological sites and monuments in the district as a whole.'

Mrs J. White, learning support assistant, Frome

'Industrial archaeological sites including Fussell's Ironworks; St Cuthbert's Smelting Works; Charterhouse lead-smelting flues.'

Mr and Mrs P. Roake, both about 80 (became interested in the Mendips at Sidcot School, 1928/32), Wells

'Industrial chimneys; rural and urban water troughs and fountains; horse mounting blocks; village pumps; stiles; unusual structures for example the summer house in Lovers Walk, Wells; old lodge properties such as those on the Kilmersdon end of the Ammerdown estate; interesting brickwork; dry-stone walling patterns which vary according to the natural material and region; and many more.'

Martyn Errington, Environmental Health Officer, Shepton Mallet

'Village churches with interesting features - sometimes redundant.'

80-year-old social history enthusiast

'The series of iron triangular-section mileposts from Glastonbury to Wells; and another from Norton St Philip; the almost intact lime-kiln south east of Lower Thrupe Farm; the crossing of five footpaths at Worminster.'

S. C. Hood, Wells

'The Hood memorial; the cedar walk; Butleigh Court; the horse trough at Butleigh Wootton; the Horse and Lion; the dovecote above Tugrushin Corner.'

Butleigh Parish Council

'Coxley pound and the Pound Inn; the Old Millhouse, Coxley (mentioned in Domesday); Hay Hill vineyard (site of medieval vineyard); Coxley cross base (late 15th century, similar to ones at Fenny Castle and Worminster); Gallows Field at Keward (site of former gallows, outside of the city boundary).'

Mrs A. Martin, local historian and archaeologist

In the Wookey area: 'The water cross at Fenny Castle; the Short Ford and Longwater Ford; groups of trees on Henley Hill and the nine cedar trees commemorating different battles in the Crimean War; Court Farm, East Court, Mellifont Abbey and other old houses that make up the village and the church; the very important green fields around the village which keep its identity and keep it separate from Wells.'

Gay and Stephen Harrison, Wookey

'Eleanor's Well. This is situated at Marston Bigot, and was the only source of fresh water for the local inhabitants. It was paid for by Eleanor Boyle, wife of the Rector of Marston Bigot, from the proceeds of her poetry and books for children. The well is shortly to undergo considerable restoration, with the legend on a plaque nearby.'

Trudoxhill Parish Council

In the Pilton area: 'The ancient part of the village bounded by the parish church to the north, the Abbey Barn to the south, the Manor House to the west and Ford Lane to the east. There is a wealth of documented history relating to this part of the village, which remains largely unspoilt providing peace, with numerous 17th/18th century buildings and several much earlier.'

Frank Challener, Pilton

In the Norton St Philip area: 'The historic splendour of the George Inn; the view from the top of the Church Mead looking across at the church and surrounding countryside; the different styles of architecture in the High Street; the walk along the lane towards Wellow; the surrounding countryside which is so important both environmentally and in keeping the village just that - a village and not part of a corridor from one town to another.'

Norton St Philip Parish Council

'The original canopy outside the Palace Theatre.'

Mr N. Mitchell, Wells

'Shepton Mallet prison. It is the oldest in the country to stand on its original site, and should be preserved. Its history is long and chequered, having been first envisaged in 1610. Many interesting features exist, and there is much historical material available.'

Francis Disney, B.E.M., author and prison historian, Shepton Mallet

LISTED BUILDINGS BY PARISH

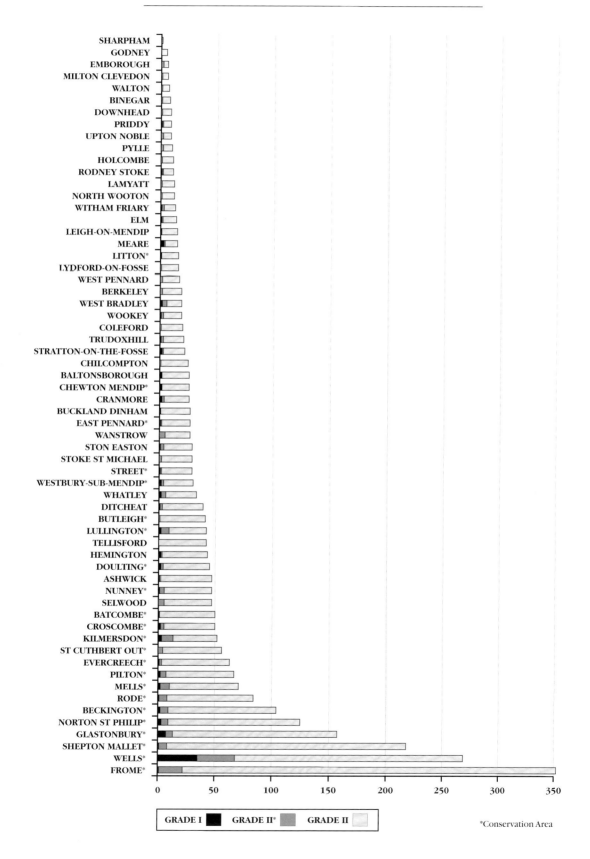

GRADE I ■	GRADE II* ▨	GRADE II ▢

*Conservation Area

SCHEDULED MONUMENTS BY PARISH

ASHWICK

Sites & Monuments Register No	Scheduled Monument No	Name	National Grid Ref
23058	238	Barrow, Beacon Hill, Ashwick	ST635462
23059	238	Barrow, Beacon Hill, Ashwick	ST635462
23060	303	Barrow, Beacon Hill, Ashwick	ST636462
23083	237	Barrow, Beacon Hill, Ashwick	ST638460

BATCOMBE

SMR No	SM No	Name	NGR
23098	438	Moated manor house site, Spargrove	ST672380

BECKINGTON

SMR No	SM No	Name	NGR
23119	29782	The Devil's Bed and Bolster, long barrow, Beckington	ST815534

BUCKLAND DINHAM

SMR No	SM No	Name	NGR
23161	256	Long barrow, Murtry Hill, Buckland Dinham	ST764507
23639	261	Murtry Old Bridge, Buckland Dinham	ST765500

BUTLEIGH

SMR No	SM No	Name	NGR
23181	448	Deserted farmstead and dovecote, Butleigh Wood, Butleigh	ST508336
23193	447	New Ditch, Butleigh Wood, Butleigh	ST506333

CHEWTON MENDIP

SMR No	SM No	Name	NGR
23206	13883	Bowl barrow, 450m SE of Red Quar Farm, Chewton Mendip	ST566517
23207	13882	Bowl barrow, 520m SE of Red Quar Farm, Chewton Mendip	ST566517
23215	13924	Bowl barrow, 300m W of Newlands Farm, Green Ore	ST571506
23216	13923	Bowl barrow, 570m W of Newlands Farm, Green Ore	ST574507
23219	472	Round barrow, W of Mendip Farm, Chewton Mendip	ST585505
23220	472	Round barrow, W of Mendip Farm, Chewton Mendip	ST585505
23222	82	Barrow, Stockhill Wood, Chewton Mendip	ST563508
23223	82	Barrow, Stockhill Wood, Chewton Mendip	ST563508
23224	123	Barrow or mound, Stockhill Wood, Chewton Mendip	ST557516
23231	13921	Barrow cemetery, Stockhill, Chewton Mendip	ST558511
23234	22804	Bowl barrow, Stockhill, Chewton Mendip	ST558511
23237	22853	Bowl barrow, Stockhill, Chewton Mendip	ST557510
23242	13860	Bowl barrow, 300m SW of Harptree Lodge, Chewton Mendip	ST536523
23243	13822	Barrow, North Hill, Chewton Mendip	ST539518
23244	13822	Barrow, North Hill, Chewton Mendip	ST539518
23245	122	Round barrow, Chewton Mendip Warren, Chewton Mendip	ST547517
23246	122	Round barrow, Chewton Mendip Warren, Chewton Mendip	ST549518
23247	122	Round barrow, Chewton Mendip Warren, Chewton Mendip	ST549515
23248	13885	Long barrow, 370m SSE of Castle Farm, Chewton Mendip	ST546526
23252	13884	Long barrow, 230m E of Chewton Plot, Chewton Mendip	ST612530
23254	13925	Long barrow, 180m N of Lime House, Chewton Mendip	ST601531
23256	13927	Barrow cemetery, Barrow House Farm, Chewton Mendip	ST602534
23260	13926	Bowl barrow, 70m E of Barrow House Farm, Chewton Mendip	ST602533
23812	13824	Ashen Hill barrow cemetery, Chewton Mendip	ST540521

CHILCOMPTON

SMR No	SM No	Name	NGR
23292	29032	Iron-age promontory fort, Blacker's Hill, Chilcompton	ST637501

CRANMORE

SMR No	SM No	Name	NGR
23324	29781	Bowl barrow, WSW of West Cranmore, Cranmore	ST659427
23325	29781	Bell barrow, WSW of West Cranrnore, Cranmore	ST659427
23326	29781	Bell barrow, WSW of West Cranmore, Cranmore	ST658427

CROSCOMBE

SMR No	SM No	Name	NGR
23349	29033	Maesbury Castle hillfort, Croscombe	ST611472
24916	29766	Village cross, Croscombe	ST591444

DITCHEAT

SMR No	SM No	Name	NGR
23380	391	Roman building, SW of Lower Sutton Farm, Ditcheat	ST618334
24915	43	Bolter's Bridge, Hornblotton	ST607334

DOULTING

SMR No	SM No	Name	NGR
23394	237	Barrow, Beacon Hill, Doulting	ST639460
23395	237	Barrow, Beacon Hill, Doulting	ST639460
23396	237	Tree ring enclosure, Beacon Hill, Doulting	ST639460
23397	265	Barrow, Beacon Hill, Doulting	ST641460
24912	29768	Wayside cross, Bodden	ST640441
24913	23	Tithe barn, Manor Farm, Doulting	ST648431

DOWNHEAD

SMR No	SM No	Name	NGR
23428	335	Dinies Camp, Downhead	ST677459

ELM

SMR No	SM No	Name	NGR
23442	369	Tedbury Camp, Elm	ST745489

EMBOROUGH

SMR No	SM No	Name	NGR
23455	13941	Barrow, NNE of Whitnell Corner	ST599491
23456	13941	Barrow, NNE of Whitnell Corner	ST599491
23457	22916	Barrow, NE of Whitnell Corner	ST599491
23458	13940	Barrow, N of Whitnell Corner	ST598493
23459	13939	Barrow, NW of Burnt Wood, Whitnell Corner	ST599496
23462	22807	Bell barrow, S of Blackwell Tyning Plantation, Emborough	ST607503
23463	471	Barrow, SSE of Redhill Farm, Emborough	ST607507

EVERCREECH

SMR No	SM No	Name	NGR
23483	257	Small Down Camp, Evercreech	ST667407
24910	29765	Churchyard cross, Evercreech	ST650387

FROME

SMR No	SM No	Name	NGR
23551	489	Dye works and drying house, Frome	ST778483
23553	489	Dye works and drying house, Willow Vale, Frome	ST779482

GLASTONBURY

SMR No	SM No	Name	NGR
23564	402	Ponters Ball (linear earthwork), Havyatt	ST535383
23570	427	Beckery chapel and cemetery, Glastonbury	ST485384
23575	235	Hospital of St Mary, chapel and men's almshouses, Glastonbury	ST499387
23605	231	Church of St Michael, The Tor, Glastonbury	ST513387
25547	1	Glastonbury Abbey, Glastonbury	ST501387
24917	22075	The Tribunal, Glastonbury	ST500390
24918	22	Tithe barn, Glastonbury	ST504386

GODNEY

SMR No	SM No	Name	NGR
23637	406	Glastonbury Lake Village, Godney	ST494409
24266	27983	Duck decoy, SE of Manor Farm, Godney	ST479416

HEMINGTON

SMR No	SM No	Name	NGR
23655	478	Roman villa and earthworks, W of Lower Row Farm, Hemington	ST763533

LAMYATT

SMR No	SM No	Name	NGR
23726	498	Shrunken medieval village, W of Speeds Farm, Lamyatt	ST653359
23728	327	Roman temple, Lamyatt Beacon, Lamyatt	ST670362
23860	29780	Hillfort, Fox Covert, Milton Clevedon	ST667368

MEARE

SMR No	SM No	Name	NGR
23552	27981	Sweet Track, Meare	ST430418
23782	22802	Abbot's fish house and fishponds, Meare	ST459418
23784	349	Iron-age settlement (Meare West), Meare	ST444423
23789	27790	Abbot's Way trackway, Westhay	ST420426
23789	27992	Abbot's Way trackway, Westhay	ST428423
23790	27992	Honeygore trackway, W of Honeygore Farm, Meare	ST421428
24262	27973	Duck decoy, N of Meare Pool, Meare	ST459431
24277	349	Iron-age settlement (Meare East), Meare	ST447422

MELLS

SMR No	SM No	Name	NGR
23442	369	Tedbury Camp, Elm	ST745489
23849	143	Kingsdown Camp, Mells Down, Mells	ST719518
23850	368	Wadbury Hillfort, Wadbury	ST736490
25394	13264	Limekiln Hill quarry cave, Mells	ST731487

MILTON CLEVEDON

SMR No	SM No	Name	NGR
23860	29780	Hillfort at Fox Covert, Milton Clevedon	ST667368

NORTON ST PHILIP

SMR No	SM No	Name	NGR
23873	252	Falconry, Lodge Farm, Farleigh Hungerford	ST797581
23878	291	Dovecote, Manor Farm, Norton St Philip	ST772560
23881	28840	Farleigh Hungerford Castle, Farleigh Hungerford	ST802578

NUNNEY

SMR No	SM No	Name	NGR
23897	22077	Nunney Castle, Nunney	ST737458
23900	282	Roman villa, Whatley Combe, Nunney	ST745470

PILTON

SMR No	SM No	Name	NGR
23918	14	Tithe barn, Pilton	ST590407

PRIDDY

SMR No	SM No	Name	NGR
23015	508	Lead works, Charterhouse	ST489549
23021	219	Roman settlement at Town Field, Charterhouse	ST499563
23024	220	Roman fort, E of, Charterhouse	ST505558
23025	218	Roman amphitheatre, Charterhouse	ST499566
23946	29036	Roman building, E of church, Priddy	ST532515
23948	13838	Bowl barrow, 130m W of church, Priddy	ST527515
23949	13839	Priddy Glebe barrow, bowl barrow, 25m N of church, Priddy	ST529515
23951	13823	Priddy Nine Barrows cemetery, North Hill, Priddy	ST540515
23960	13829	Bowl barrow, 500m N of East Water, Priddy	ST538515
23964	13880	Bowl barrow, 230m NW of Hunters Lodge Inn, Priddy	ST548502
23966	13836	Bowl barrow, 310m SE of Eastwater Farm, East Water	ST538506
23971	13843	Long barrow, 600m ENE of Brimble Pit Pool, Priddy	ST515510
23972	13842	Bowl barrow, 750m SW of Dale Farm, Priddy Green	ST520509
23975	13845	Bowl barrow, 770m SW of Townsend Farm, Priddy	ST517512
23976	13846	Bowl barrow, 800m SW of Townsend Farm, Priddy	ST518512
23977	13847	Bowl barrow, 850m SW of Townsend Farm, Priddy	ST518511
23980	13844	Linear barrow cemetery, 510m SW of Townsend Pool, Priddy	ST516517
23990	13818	Bowl barrow, S730m SE of Bristol Plain Farm, Priddy	ST510517
23991	13819	Bowl barrow, 760m SE of Bristol Plain Farm, Priddy	ST510517
23992	13820	Bowl barrow, 810m SE of Bristol Plain Farm, Priddy	ST511517
23993	13821	Bowl barrow, 850m SE of Bristol Plain Farm, Priddy	ST511517
23995	13814	Bowl barrow, 390m NE of Bristol Plain Farm, Priddy	ST507523
23996	13815	Bowl barrow, 410m NE of Bristol Plain Farm, Priddy	ST508522
23997	13816	Bowl barrow, 420m E of Bristol Plain Farm, Priddy	ST508522
23998	13817	Bowl barrow, 450m E of Bristol Plain Farm, Priddy	ST508521
24002	13825	Barrow, 600m E of Priddy Hill Farm, Priddy	ST521529
24003	13853	Bowl barrow, 70m W of Rowberrow Farm, Priddy	ST521522
24004	13854	Bowl barrow, 70m NW of Hill View, Priddy	ST522524
24005	13855	Rowberrow: bowl barrow 40m N of Hill View, Priddy	ST523524
24006	13856	Bowl barrow, 90m NE of Hill View, Priddy	ST523524
24010	13831	Bowl barrow, 460m E of Charterhouse Warren Farm, Priddy	ST505549
24011	13932	Bowl barrow, SE of Charterhouse Warren Farm, Priddy	ST506549
24013	22806	Bowl barrow, 365m SW of Ubley Warren Farm, Priddy	ST512550
24014	13929	Bowl barrow, 250m NE of King Down Farm, Priddy	ST510544
24015	13930	Bowl barrow, 70m NE of King Down Farm, Priddy	ST509542
24016	13931	Bowl barrow, 180m SW of Yoxter Farm, Priddy	ST511539
24017	13848	Bowl barrow, 430m NW of King Down Farm, Priddy	ST504543
24018	13850	Bowl barrow, 430m SW of King Down Farm, Priddy	ST504540
24019	13849	Bowl barrow, 150m SW of King Down Farm, Priddy	ST507541
24020	13827	Barrow, 350m NE of Cheddar Head Farm, Priddy	ST505531
24022	13936	Bowl barrow, 260m E of Templedown Farm, Priddy	ST519549
24023	13937	Bowl barrow, 340m E of Templedown Farm, Priddy	ST520549
24026	13826	Stow barrow: bowl barrow 700m SW of Haydon Grange Farm, Priddy	ST521536
24034	13857	Bowl barrow, 320m E of Lodmore Farm, Priddy	ST536540
24035	13858	Bowl barrow, 510m SE of Lodmore Farm, Priddy	ST538538
24036	13859	Bowl barrow, 570m SE of Lodmore Farm, Priddy	ST538537
24037	13862	Bowl barrow, 450m NW of Harptree Lodge, Priddy	ST534529
24139	13861	Bowl barrow, 350m NW of Harptree Lodge, Priddy	ST535528
24041	29040	Barrow, E of Harptree Lodge, Priddy	ST541525
24042	29037	Priddy Circle, SW of Castle of Comfort Inn, Priddy	ST540526
24043	29037	Priddy Circle, SW of Castle of Comfort Inn, Priddy	ST541528
24044	29037	Mound, Priddy Circle, Priddy	ST541529
24045	29037	Priddy Circle, SW of Castle of Comfort Inn, Priddy	ST541531
24046	29041	Priddy Circle, N of Castle of Comfort Inn, Priddy	ST543536
24050	29041	Barrow, E of Hill Grange, Priddy	ST542536
24054	124	Barrow, SE of Castle of Comfort Inn, Priddy	ST546530
24055	136	Barrow, N of Lodmore Farm, Priddy	ST534545
24056	136	Barrow, NW of Pool Farm, Priddy	ST534547
24057	136	Barrow, NW of Pool Farm, Priddy	ST536547
24058	136	Barrow, NW of Pool Farm, Priddy	ST537547
24059	136	Barrow, Wright's Piece, S of Fernhill Farm, Priddy	ST530549
24060	136	Barrow, Wright's Piece, S of Fernhill Farm, Priddy	ST531548
24061	136	Barrow, Wright's Piece, S of Fernhill Farm, Priddy	ST531548
24062	136	Barrow, SE of Wright's Piece, S of Fernhill Farm, Priddy	ST532548
24063	136	Barrow, N of Haydon Grange, Priddy	ST526547
24064	136	Barrow, N of Haydon Grange, Priddy	ST527547
24065	136	Bell barrow, N of Haydon Grange, Priddy	ST528547
24066	136	Barrow, N of Haydon Grange, Priddy	ST529546
24069	13863	Bowl barrow, 220m SW of Ubley Hill Farm, Priddy	ST516573
24070	13865	Bowl barrow, 370m E of Ubley Hill Farm, Priddy	ST522574
24071	13864	Bowl barrow, 280m SE of Ubley Hill Farm, Priddy	ST520574
24075	13866	Bowl barrow, 300m N of Hazel Manor, Priddy	ST528571
24079	13928	Bowl barrow, 550m SW of Nordrach, Priddy	ST508558
24080	22805	Bowl barrow, 180m W of Ubley Warren Farm, Priddy	ST511553
24083	13934	Barrow, 400m NW of Starve Lark Farm, Priddy	ST531561

24084	13935	Barrow, 250m W of Starve Lark Farm, Priddy	ST533560
24085	13869	Bowl barrow, 390m NW of Fernhill Farm, Priddy	ST525558
24086	13870	Bowl barrow, 350m NW of Fernhill Farm, Priddy	ST526558
24087	13938	Bowl barrow, 610m NW of Whitestown Farm, Priddy	ST523553
24088	13868	Bowl barrow, 450m SW of Fernhill Farm, Priddy	ST525553
24089	13867	Bowl barrow, 20m NW of Whitestown Farm, Priddy	ST528553
24095	13832	Barrow, 870m SW of Charterhouse Warren Farm, Priddy	ST493546
24096	13833	Barrow, 340m NE of Wellington Farm, Priddy	ST493541
24100	13942	Bowl barrow, 700m SW of Middle Ellick Farm, Priddy	ST490570
24101	13943	Bowl barrow, 590m SW of Middle Ellick Farm, Priddy	ST491571
24103	13902	Barrow, Beacon Batch, Priddy	ST484573
24104	13903	Disc barrow, Beacon Batch, Priddy	ST485574
24105	13903	Barrow, Beacon Batch, Priddy	ST485573
24106	13903	Barrow, Beacon Batch, Priddy	ST485573
24107	13903	Barrow, Beacon Batch, Priddy	ST486573
24108	13903	Barrow, Beacon Batch, Priddy	ST486573
24109	13904	Barrow, Beacon Batch, Priddy	ST487572
24110	13905	Barrow, Beacon Batch, Priddy	ST485572
24111	13905	Barrow, Beacon Batch, Priddy	ST485571
24112	25007	Barrow, Beacon Batch, Priddy	ST486572
24113	13907	Barrow, Beacon Batch, Priddy	ST485572
24115	108	Barrow, Black Down, Priddy	ST474572
24116	108	Barrow, Black Down, Priddy	ST474572
24117	108	Barrow, Black Down, Priddy	ST474571
24137	13834	Barrow, 170m SE of Hunters Lodge Inn, Priddy	ST551501
24140	13840	Disc barrow, 610m NE of Drove Cottage, Priddy	ST560501
24143	13837	Bowl barrow, 600m N of Rookham Plantation, Rookham	ST546492
24145	13835	Barrow, SW of Hunters Lodge Inn, Priddy	ST541495
24151	13830	Bowl barrow, 300m SW of Moor View, Priddy	ST522494
24152	13828	Bowl barrow, 400m SW of Moor View, Priddy	ST520494
24153	13874	Bowl barrow, 380m SE of Southfield Farm, Priddy	ST552497
24154	29764	Henge, 370m NE of Drove Cottage, Priddy	ST560499
24156	13872	Bowl barrow, 470m SE of Southfield Farm, Priddy	ST555498
24157	13871	Bowl barrow, 550m SE of Southfield Farm, Pnddy	ST556498
24158	13873	Bowl barrow, 570m SE of Southfield Farm, Priddy	ST556497
24159	124	Barrow, W end of the Belt, Priddy	ST552528
24228	24228	Bowl barrow, 870m SW of Dale Farm, Priddy Green	ST518510

RODE

SMR No	SM No	Name	NGR
24251	269	Rode Bridge, Rode	ST803544

RODNEY STOKE

SMR No	SM No	Name	NGR
24268	492	Deserted farmstead and associated field system, Rodney Stoke	ST490517
24269	29039	Westbury Camp hillfort, N of Stoke Woods, Rodney Stoke	ST493512
24271	13910	Bowl barrow, 330m N of Stoke Woods, Rodney Stoke	ST492514
24272	13911	Bowl barrow, 400m N of Stoke Woods, Rodney Stoke	ST495513
24273	13912	Bowl barrow, 430m NE of Stoke Woods, Rodney Stoke	ST498512
24279	22915	Bowl barrow, 900m SW of Bristol Plain Farm, Rodney Stoke	ST496515
24280	29039	Barrow, Westbury Camp, Rodney Stoke	ST493512
24282	13913	Bowl barrow, 420m N of Stoke Woods, Rodney Stoke	ST494514
24283	22809	Romano-British settlement site, Stoke Moor	ST461491
24286	13914	Barrow, 820m S of Bristol Plain Farm, Rodney Stoke	ST505512
24287	13915	Barrow, 550m S of Bristol Plain Farm, Rodney Stoke	ST503515
24288	13916	Bowl barrow, 640m S of Bristol Plain Farm, Rodney Stoke	ST503514
24289	13916	Bowl barrow, 640m S of Bristol Plain Farm, Rodney Stoke	ST503514
24290	13908	Bowl barrow, 700m S of Bristol Plain Farm, Rodney Stoke	ST504513

SELWOOD

SMR No	SM No	Name	NGR
24459	495	Marston deserted village, N of Lower Marston, Selwood	ST770448
24461	24021	Hales Castle, E of Woodlands, Selwood	ST798443
24462	24020	Roddenbury Hillfort, Longleat Wood, Selwood	ST799440
24463	390	Roman settlement, SW of St Algar's Farm, Selwood	ST785419

SHARPHAM

SMR No	SM No	Name	NGR
24263	27968	Duck decoy, SE of Ham Wall Rhyne, Sharpham	ST468404
24493	27971	Duck decoy in Sharpham Park, Sharpham	ST464383
25545	27975	Tinney's trackways, W of Sharpham Bridge, Sharpham	ST468382

SHEPTON MALLET

SMR No	SM No	Name	NGR
24914	175	The Shambles, Market Place, Shepton Mallet	ST620437
25160	22803	Roman Town, Shepton Mallet	ST630426

ST CUTHBERT OUT

SMR No	SM No	Name	GR
24311	92	Foard barrow, Green Ore	ST577504
24312	92	Barrow, Green Ore	ST577504
24331	13266	Outlook Cave	ST525487
24334	13267	Bracelet Cave	ST523484
24336	24024	King's Castle enclosures, Iron-age defended settlement, Wells	ST569457
24337	89A	Barrow, S of Beechbarrow, St Cuthbert Out	ST571490
24339	89B	Barrow site, E of Beechbarrow, St Cuthbert Out	ST575489
24340	88	Barrow site, SE of Hill Grove, St Cuthbert Out	ST579491
24341	88	Barrow, E of Haydon Hill Farm, St Cuthbert Out	ST579490
24342	88	Barrow, E of Haydon Hill Farm, St Cuthbert Out	ST580490
24351	90	Long barrow site, E of Hill Grove, St Cuthbert Out	ST586497
24352	90	Barrow site, E of Hill Grove, St Cuthbert Out	ST587496
24354	13257	Badger Hole cave, Wookey Hole	ST533480
24356	86	Long barrow, Penn Hill, St Cuthbert Out	ST564487
24357	86	Barrow, Pen Hill, St Cuthbert Without	ST564487
24358	86	Cairn, Pen Hill, St Cuthbert Out	ST565488
24363	87	Cairn or barrow, Big Plantation, St Cuthbert Out	ST568486
24364	87	Barrow, Big Plantation, St Cuthbert Out	ST567486
24365	87	Barrow, Big Plantation, St Cuthbert Out	ST567485
24366	85	Barrow or mound, NW of Pen Hill Farm, St Cuthbert Out	ST554485
24374	83	Barrow cemetery, N of Pen Hill Wood, St Cuthbert Out	ST558487
24376	29775	Bowl barrow, 400m S of Rookham, Rookham	ST553493
24377	29763	Bowl barrow, Whitnell Corner, St Cuthbert Out	ST597487
24378	29762	Bowl barrow, Whitnell Corner, St Cuthbert Out	ST594487
24384	94	Barrow, NW of Green Ore, St Cuthbert Out	ST573503
24398	84	Barrows or clearance mounds, N of Rookham Cottage, St Cuthbert Out	ST542488
24451	13258	Rhinoceros Hole cave, Wookey Hole	ST533480
24905	91	Barrow, Horrington Hill, St Cuthbert Out	ST583481
24906	91	Barrow, Horrington Hill, St Cuthbert Out	ST579480
25360	13265	Savory's Hole	ST529489

STOKE ST MICHAEL

SMR No	SM No	Name	NGR
24956	13263	Browne's Hole cave, S of Cook's Wood, Stoke St Michael	ST670476

STON EASTON

SMR No	SM No	Name	NGR
24974	449	Barrow, N of Home Farm Cottage, Ston Easton	ST622543

STREET

SMR No	SM No	Name	NGR
24708	274	Roman villa, Marshall's Elm, Street	ST489347
25522	27984	Medieval causeway, N of Street	ST488376

TRUDOXHILL

SMR No	SM No	Name	NGR
24736	29779	Marston Moat, S of Moat Farm, Trudoxhill	ST768439

WALTON

SMR No	SM No	Name	NGR
24759	27969	Decoy, near Eighteen Feet Rhyne, Walton	ST448344
24760	27970	Decoy, Walton Moor, Walton	ST458338
24761	27967	Decoy, Walton Moor, Walton	ST461339

WANSTROW

SMR No	SM No	Name	NGR
24775	436	Prehistoric earthwork, N of Stubbs Wood, Merehead	ST696438

WELLS

SMR No	SM No	Name	NGR
23034	240	St Andrew's Well and well house, E of Cathedral, Wells	ST553459
24798	24	Bishop's Tithe Barn, Wells	ST551456
25370	240	Bishop's Palace, Wells	ST553458
25371	233	Brown's Gate, Wells	ST550459

WESTBURY-SUB-MENDIP

SMR No	SM No	Name	NGR
24254	27965	Duck decoy, E of Westbury	ST479485
24791	29769	Westbury village cross, Westbury	ST501489
24839	29772	Barrow, S of Brimble Pit Pool, Westbury	ST509505
24840	29772	Barrow, S of Brimble Pit Pool, Westbury	ST509505
24841	263	Barrow, ENE of Westbury Beacon, Westbury	ST503509
24842	263	Barrow, ENE of Westbury Beacon, Westbury	ST504509
24843	29770	Barrow, NE of Foxhills Wood, Westbury	ST512504
24845	29771	Barrow or cairn, W of Foxhills Wood, Westbury	ST513501
24846	29771	Barrow or cairn, E of Foxhills Wood, Westbury	ST513501
24848	263	Westbury Beacon (barrow), Westbury	ST501508
24851	13909	Bowl barrow, 850m S of Bristol Plain Farm, Westbury	ST505512
25675	463	Deserted medieval farmstead and field system	ST515493

WITHAM FRIARY

SMR No	SM No	Name	NGR
24892	357	Carthusian Priory, house and garden, Witham Hall Farm, Witham Friary	ST759417

WOOKEY

SMR No	SM No	Name	NGR
23002 (Multi-parish site)	22808	Post-Roman settlement and monastic site, Marchey Farm, Bleadney	ST479464
23005	27961	Bishop's Palace and dovecote, Wookey	ST518458
24232	29767	Fenny Castle Cross, Castle	ST509441
24455	29035	Fenny Castle (motte & bailey), North Moor, St Cuthbert Out	ST509436

INDEX

83